The Perspective
of Women's Entrepreneurship
in the Age of Globalization

The Perspective of Women's Entrepreneurship in the Age of Globalization

Edited by

Mirjana Radović Marković
Akamai University

INFORMATION AGE PUBLISHING, INC.
Charlotte, NC • www.infoagepub.com

Library of Congress Cataloging-in-Publication Data

The perspective of women's entrepreneurship in the age of globalization /
edited by Mirjana Radović.
    p. cm.
 Includes bibliographical references.
 ISBN-13: 978-1-59311-769-6 (pbk.)
 ISBN-13: 978-1-59311-770-2 (hardcover)
 1. Businesswomen. 2. Self-employed women. 3. Women-owned business
enterprises. 4. Entrepreneurship. 5. Globalization. I. Radović, Mirjana.
 HD6072.5.P47 2007
 338'.04082–dc22

                                                        2007023852

*This book is dedicated to prof. Dr. Kenneth Gray (55),
who has early and suddenly passed away on 24 March 2007,
one month after we had completed our book. He died after reaching
the top of a rock face he was climbing. Touching the top of the rock
he touched the stars and became one of the shinest star in the sky.
Dr. Gray will be truly missed like a great professor, colleague,
and a wonderful person.*

*Thanks again for your trust to this project and your support
to me and my work.*

Dr. Mirjana Radović Marković

Editor-in-Chief

Professor Mirjana Radović Marković, PhD is a professor of Entrepreneurship and director of the Masters program, "Entrepreneurship for Women," at Akamai University, Hilo, HI and Principal Research Fellow at the Institute of Economic Sciences in Belgrade, Serbia.

Reviewers of the Book

Professor Kenneth R. Gray, PhD
Eminent Scholar Chair of Global Business
Professor of International Management
School of Business and Industry
Florida A & M University
Tallahassee, Florida.

Professor Douglas Capogrossi, PhD
President of the Akamai University
Hilo, HI

Language Editor

Eugenia Onwu Ukpo, PhD,
Assistant Director
Department of Academic Support Services
NTI, Kaduna, Nigeria

CONTENTS

Introduction ix

PART I

**Small Businesses as an Opportunity for Women to Add
A New Professional Dimension to the Traditional Role
in the Family and Society**

1   **The Change of Women's Roles through the Centuries:
Confrontation of Tradition with New Challenges**. 3
Mirjana Radović Marković

2   **Past Female Entrepreneurship with the Stress on the Future
in New Economy Globalization** 13
Maika Valencia

3   **Cultivating Entrepreneurship among Women
in the 21st Century**. 25
Olugbenga Adesanya

PART II

**Women Entrepreneurs, Managers, and Leaders:
Challenges and Opportunities in Developed, Developing,
and Transitional Economies**

4   **La Vita Imprenditoriale: Female and Male Entrepreneurs
in Italy** 41
Siri Terjesen and Vanessa Ratten

5   **Women Entrepreneurs in Morocco: Vanguards of Change
in the Muslim World** 55
Kenneth R. Gray and Doris H. Gray

6 Women Entrepreneurs and Development in Nigeria............ 69
Priscilla M. Achakpa

7 Women Entrepreneurs and Managers in Serbia 77
Mirjana Radović Marković

8 Women Leaders: Case Study of Serbia 87
Mirjana Radović Marković

9 Leading Women Entrepreneurs of Thailand 95
Siri Terjesen, Caroline Hatcher, Tatiana Wysocki, and Jessica Pham

10 Women Entrepreneurship Context in Latin America:
An Exploratory Study in Chile 109
José Ernesto Amorós and Olga Pizarro Stiepović

PART III

Suitable Financial Arrangements That
Support Female Entrepreneurship

11 Do Women Benefit from Microcredit 129
Aneel Karnani

12 Diversity Pays Financially 137
Murad Ali

PART IV

Empowering Women through Education

13 Virtual Faculties: The Education of the Future 149
Mirjana Radović Marković and DuΩan Marković

14 Community Education, Women, and Entrepreneurship 157
Isiaka Esema

15 Ensuring Quality for Nontraditional Universities and Colleges ... 171
Douglass Capogrossi

16 Women in Distance Education in Nigeria 177
Eugenia Onwu Ukpo

17 Muslim Women Education in Kenya 185
Najwa Gadaheldam

ACKNOWLEDGEMENTS

My appreciation goes to all of the chapter authors who showed interest in this project and contributed with their research papers. With their contribution, this project confirmed its international character, by including a great number of experts in the field of women entrepreneurship from various parts of the world—Europe, United States, South America, Australia, Africa, and Asia. Undisputed is the help of my highly respected colleagues, professor Dr. Kenneth Gray and professor Dr. Douglass Capogrossi, who have reviewed the book and gave me useful suggestions.

I am especially indebted to my dear colleague, Dr. Siri Terjesen, who did with her team of professors and experts two research papers for this book.

Additionally, I am particularly grateful to Dr. Eugenia Upko for language editing the manuscript into a readable form.

If this volume helps in any way to make the world for women's initiatives a better place in the age of globalization, then we shall be well content.

—Professor Mirjana Radović Marković, PhD
February 2007

INTRODUCTION

This book, *The Perspective of Women's Entrepreneurship in the Age of Globalization,* addresses the issue of female entrepreneurship development in the context of globalization. The authors take the position that entrepreneurship serves as a catalyst of economic development and the globalization process has progressively reduced barriers to entrepreneurship and increased competition in the global market. Namely, important settings of intercountry cooperation in our times are the emergence of the phenomenon of globalization. Like an oncoming vehicle, globalization cannot be stopped. However, we can influence its direction and we can prepare to use it as an instrument for improving the conditions of the greater majority of people all over the world. The recognition of the capacity of women entrepreneurs in our global community is no longer a matter for debate. It is our reality that female entrepreneurship has been the major factor contributing to the development of many countries.

Today's world is changing at a startling pace. Political and economic transformations seem to be occurring everywhere. These changes have created economic opportunities for women who want to own and operate businesses. Therefore, women are increasingly choosing business ownership as a career path. As a result, women in advanced market economies and developed countries today own more than 25% of all business and have improved their position in the business world. Some of the countries are leaders by the number of newly founded women's organizations. The goal of these organizations is to gather women business owners regardless of the size of their businesses. However, in some regions of the world, transformation to a market economy threatens to sharpen gender inequality. Some of these changes are simply the legacy of a gender imbalance that existed prior to political and economic reform. Other changes reflect a return to traditional norms and values that relegated women to a secondary status. Namely, the social, cultural, and traditional taboos on women in these regions and countries allow men to carve legitimacy for themselves in public affairs, as well as in the sphere of production and related economic activity. In other words, women entrepreneurs are seen in subordinate roles. As countries become more democratic, gender in equalities lessen, thus offering a more productive atmosphere for both sexes. In other words, by overcoming (recidivism of still) existing prejudices, customs, and opinions, they have to fight not only to be recognized as women-mothers, but also as women- leaders, in order to gain an equal place in the business game with men.

The purpose of this book is to explore the following:

1. How small businesses can be an opportunity for women to add a new professional dimension to their traditional role in the family and society

2. Concepts and models for combining career and family

3. The role of women in the development of the private sector in the 21st century

4. The support required for women to undertake a business activity (e.g., availability of structures supporting women entrepreneurs such as professional female networks)

5. Suitable financial arrangements that can support female entrepreneurship (e.g., proximity of financing programs from traditional banks, microcredit organizations, etc.)

6. New educational opportunities for women determination of educational level and degree of entrepreneurial skills/distance education opportunities

7. The specific country needs: transition economies, developed and developing economies

8. How to provide realistic incentives for women to take their businesses global

This book brings together a large amount of information on various women entrepreneurship opportunities from different points of view and from different countries and regions. The special value of this volume is the networking of researchers-scientists and other professionals and experts all over the world and their participation with the articles based on research undertaken specifically for the book.

The book has international character, which presents in one place the state of the matter in the field of women entrepreneurship at the beginning of the 21st century in developing, developed, and transitional economies. A number of case studies highlight specific examples of women's entrepreneurship around the world. Covering a wide selection of countries and methodological approaches, the papers aim to provide global perspective on a variety of possible approaches to female entrepreneurship research.

Additionally, this book provides important recommendations. The first set of recommendations focuses on the development of women's entrepreneurship at a local and regional level. The second set of recommendations underlines the objective limits that still hinder women from going into business (i.e., with a stress on how societal, cultural, and religious attitudes impede women in business). The third set of recommendations highlights the need to promote and strengthen the potential for enhancing women entrepreneurship on the global level and support networks of women dealing with business. Additionally, its goal was to offer ways of encouraging entrepreneurship, including the role of the education system, developing positive attitudes, and an active approach toward female entrepreneurship.

This book contains four parts that are made up of 18 chapters.

The first part of the book is titled, "Small Businesses as an Opportunity for Women to Add a New Professional Dimension to the Traditional Role in Family and Society." In Chapters 1–3, the authors focus on women in the context of history. They explain how the role of women has changed throughout the ages, with emphasis on the perspective of women's entrepreneurship in the Age of Globalization.

The second part of the book, "Women Entrepreneurs, Managers, and Leaders: Challenges and Opportunities in Developed, Developing, and Transitional Economies in Europe, Africa, Asia, and Latin America." The authors in this section examine the nature and extent of female entrepreneurship in relation to the role of women in the aforementioned regions. This includes Chapters 4–10, which provide new insights into the involvement of women entrepreneurs and their contribution to economic and social development in these economies. The section allows for comparisons and conclusions with respect to female entrepreneurship in countries with differing political, religious, economic environments and cultural backgrounds. All of the country chapters are empirically grounded using original research.

The third part of the book is titled "Suitable Financial Arrangements that Support Female Entrepreneurship." The first author in this section considers the role of microfinance in empowering female entrepreneurship and reducing poverty in chapter twelve. Additionally, the second article, chapter thirteen, is devoted to diversity in the workforce and its financial impact on firms. The both papers have critical approaches to the topic.

The fourth part of the book, "Empowering Women through Education," Chapters 14–18, examines new educational opportunities for women in the era of new technology and globalization. The chapter authors focus their research on education, due to the increasingly important role of knowledge and education in the last decade. In other words, the exchange of knowledge is paramount because of the pervasive effects of globalization. Thus, technology and the Internet have aided globalization, and helped lessen the gap between the rich and the poor as well as the gap between women and men.

Finally, *The Perspective of Women's Entrepreneurship in the Age of Globalization* provides a foundation for further study of women entrepreneurship and globalization. It appeals to scholars and students in development studies, women's studies, international business and economics. This collection of insightful articles ties together the streams of thought on women entrepreneurship worldwide.

—Mirjana Radović Marković, PhD

PART I

**SMALL BUSINESSES AS AN OPPORTUNITY
FOR WOMEN TO ADD A NEW PROFESSIONAL
DIMENSION TO THE TRADITIONAL ROLE
IN THE FAMILY AND SOCIETY**

THE CHANGE OF WOMEN'S ROLES THROUGH THE CENTURIES

Confrontation of Tradition with New Challenges

Mirjana Radović Marković

INTRODUCTION

For women, it has been a long struggle for self-realization as an exemplary mother and male companion, and respected businessperson. Traditionally, women did not receive appropriate support from the family, which acknowledged and rewarded only the traditional gender roles. Women in business were lonely and misunderstood, often disapproved in their intentions to prove themselves equally qualified and worthy among men.

As established models of society slowly evolved from the male-centered paradigm in business leadership, women established numerous global associations, whose mission was to fight for women's right to work and share equally in the benefits of culture. Usually women in these movements were unjustly characterized as "mannish" or with "excess of male hormones."

The Perspective of Women's Entrepreneurship in the Age of Globalization, pages 3–11
Copyright © 2007 by Information Age Publishing

They were marked as deviant, not because of their need to be different from their mothers, but because they wanted to replace the kitchen and apron with the office, cellular telephone, and other modern gadgets of daily work.

Women who managed to struggle against the prevailing worldview, to successfully join the modern social flows in the new way, were not fairly rewarded for their work, most times being paid less for their work than their male counterparts at the same level. They were stepped over in promotions and disrespected within the employment hierarchy. They were given undistinguished and lower status functions, and for the most part, denied any real opportunity to show their true talents. Instead, women's role in the business world was unjustly marginalized, which diminished their capabilities to creatively participate in business decision making within their companies.

Those women who were most persistent in fighting for their rightful place in business and wished to cross the traditional gender boundaries often paid the greatest price. They were forced to renounce their right to start a family, and because of the expectations of the upper levels of business, it was most often impossible to balance both business and family responsibilities. Thus, because of society's slow response in providing social support mechanisms for working women, many committed to full-time employment turned their backs on family and suffered in their private lives, or they successfully adopted new, more popular forms of self-employment, the home business.

With time, the home business has become the most acceptable business model for women raising children who refused to renounce their engagement with their profession. These women, who select the home business option, are more effective at coordinating their roles as mother, and realizing their dreams as successful businesspersons. The success of women in home business has influenced their self-respect and self-confidence. Now these women not only contribute to the family budget, they are also enabled to remain engaged with their responsibilities in properly raising their children and functioning as a wife within the marital relationship.

Although most home businesses remain small-scale businesses, many businesses started in the home expand into the community, as the children grow and require less hands-on care. In fact, some world trends show that in the last decade of the 20th century the numbers of female managers have increased significantly. They lead many of the world's largest companies with great success, changing dramatically the image of women in contributing effectively to the overall success of business.

With this proven success, women have altered the traditional perspective of the role of women in business. With the increased participation of women in business leadership, completely new ways of business communication have been put in place, and effective new business strategies and company development models have been proven. As a consequence of women infiltrating fields of business that were traditionally men's areas, women have used their advantages, durability, and persistence in work and, above all, intuition in making business decisions, thus contributing new business advantages.

Considering this trend of increased participation by women in business leadership, it can be expected that women will have more important roles in business startups and development in many of the world's economies, in spite of continued lines of distinction between male and female occupations, even now. Nevertheless, the facts clearly demonstrate that modern businesswomen will continue to establish new marks and success, as time moves on.

WOMEN'S ENTREPRENEURIAL SPIRIT THROUGH HISTORY

Women were economically active since prehistory, although their part in the workforce varied from those days until today, depending on the structure of needs, cultural, social, and other forms of a society. In Babylon in the year 2000 BC, women raised cattle along with men. Besides that, they have been engaged in raising children, cooking, making clothes, and other similar jobs in the countryside community. Later, as cities developed, women started to work outside the house, as market traders, laundresses, courtesans, and nurses. In ancient Greece, women who belonged to the upper class did not work, which was not the case with the poor, who were usually an unqualified workforce doing the hardest job. Instead of money, they got food and accommodation. They were without any protection or rights. A similar situation was in other ancient societies. Not before the 14th century in England and France women who knew some of the crafts (tailoring, weaving, etc.) were acknowledged equally as men who were carpenters, tailors, shoemakers, and so on. With guild development, women have started to be paid directly. Many of them are working in their homes, manufacturing everything. Only in the 18th and early 19th century, during the Industrial Revolution, manufacturing started to retreat to industrial production. With the development of factories, women started to be employed in them and to be men's competitors in many ways. However, they have mostly opted for traditionally female jobs, which are less paid and less valued. Factory owners employed them in textile and similar industries because they are skilled workers, but they work for 12 or more hours and for the lowest wages. This is the example of the ultimate exploitation of the female workforce in the early capitalist system, which has not only been without any rights, but also had no union protection, as the unions represented only men.

Many years later, in 1948, the International Labor Organization (ILO) brought a Convention of the employment policy, in which all kinds of discrimination against women, including the opportunity for employment, was banned. Before this Convention, women had no rights compared to men.

In view of the change of the status of women with regards to employment, the following generalizations could be made in relation to paid work for women.

1. Women worked throughout history in order to satisfy their economic needs.
2. Poor women worked regardless of their marital status, if men could not provide enough for the family's needs.
3. Women were always responsible for the raising of their children, regardless of whether they had paid jobs or not.
4. They were usually paid less than men and had lower professional status.
5. Women's work was similar to that in their own house.

TROUBLES OF THE FIRST EDUCATED WOMEN

Agnothica was the daughter of the wealthiest man and a man of the highest standing in Athens. Accordingly, her father enabled her to study medicine and to become, according to historical sources, the first female doctor in the world. However, since the laws of that time did not allow women to study and to perform "men's jobs," she had to overcome many obstacles, from the moment she decided to study medicine to the moment when she started medical practice. In order to overcome unjust law, she cut off her hair and put on men's clothing. Disguised, she appeared as the famous doctor and professor of that time, Hyeropulous, who did not suspect anything, but liked his hard-working and clever student.

After she finished her studies, Agnothica started to practice and quickly gained many patients among women, whom she told under oath that she was a woman. Due to her great popularity and numerous patients, other doctors accused "him" of deceiving patients. In a court of law her secret was revealed, which only increased her guilt. The court sentenced her not only to prison, but also to exile. When women from Athens learned about that, they besieged Athens's Senate for 3 days, until the Senate changed the verdict. Due to their demands, Agnothica was freed from any guilt and allowed to practice medicine legally.

However, other women were not allowed to practice medicine. But at the initiative of some other female organizations, women were allowed to study and to be educated, which greatly improved their position at that time.

WOMEN'S IMPROVED POSITION IN THE LAST DECADE IN DEVELOPED COUNTRIES

In modern times, there have been greater changes in the position of women in industrially developed countries of the world. Among others, there has been an increase in the total workforce from 38% in Germany to 55% in Sweden. In addition, statistically, we can notice that there still is no parity between salaries for men and women. Among developed countries, Sweden achieved the greatest results, thus almost equalized salaries. Besides that, women in Sweden have the greatest rights and protection. Women also have equal opportunities to educate themselves and to improve and advance in their jobs. Many countries tend toward this ideal. Besides the points mentioned above, for the past few decades many things have changed between the sexes and it is not a rare thing to see a successful businesswoman who lead some of the largest and best-known companies, such as Hewlett-Packard, Boeing, or Amazon.

The expansion of businesspersons in the world and the changes in management style to which women gave new business spirit influenced the formation of numerous associations of women entrepreneurs and managers. Their goal is to allow women to connect and integrate as well as possible, both at the national and international levels.

In the developed countries of Europe, improvement of women's position is noticeable, due to the better network of their connections and the foundation of women's organizations, whose goal is to promote and initiate the development of women's entrepreneurship. Some of the countries are leaders by the number of newly founded women's organizations, like Germany and Great Britain, which have 13 women entrepreneurs' organizations. One of the best-known organizations of this kind in the world is the British Association of Women Entrepreneurs (BAWE). This is a nonprofit organization whose goal is to gather women business owners regardless of the size of their businesses. This organization enables the connection of women entrepreneurs with consultation and training.

Another very successful organization in this domain is the European Federation of Black Women Business Owners. This organization has its branches throughout Europe (in Great Britain, France, and The Netherlands). In addition, at the end of 1999 in Toronto, Canada, women entrepreneurs of Canada and America signed a contract with the intention to increase trade exchange between these two countries, in which their contribution would be greater than before. More than 250 women took active part in this Congress and also attended the signing of the mentioned document.

These meetings, apart from the aim to promote the most successful entrepreneurs, also have the task to widen business networks of women around the world. By widening these business networks, women narrow the gap that existed throughout history to determine their work engagement. However, this doesn't mean that all barriers are crossed and that on that road of self-conformation in the professional sphere they have no more struggles. By overcoming recidivisms of still existing prejudices, customs, and opinions, they have to fight not only to be recognized as women, but also as women leaders, in order to gain an equal place in the "business game" with men.

EMPOWERING WOMEN IN DEVELOPING COUNTRIES

As women entrepreneurship plays an important role in the development and growth of developed countries, the importance of promoting women in economic activities is being increasingly realized in all developing countries, too. Empowering women by bringing them into the mainstream of development and by improving their economic status and providing them with new employment opportunities for income generation, self-employment, and entrepreneurship in different socioeconomic sectors is noticeable. Experience demonstrates that there are a large number of women in most developing countries capable of and willing to be involved in economic activities. An important tool of women empowerment is micro credit, which has been accepted as an effective tool for poverty alleviation and an approach to development. Micro credits have become exceptionally popular, especially in developing economies. A specific solution for solving women's difficulties in obtaining financing has been micro financing. Micro financing appears therefore to offer a "win–win" solution, where both financial institutions and poor clients benefit (Murdoch, 1999).

Women in Africa today represent 52% of the population, which is a total of 805 million. Therefore, they should be seriously considered and investment should be made toward their education as well as in their employment in the formal sector of the economy. Micro credits are especially important for starting their own businesses, considering the increasing interest among women who tend to become or already are entrepreneurs. Studies of Yoruba women in Nigeria have revealed all of the attributes of women entrepreneurs. These women have been engaged in commercial or trading activities since precolonial times (Akinwumi, 2000). Akinwumi (2000) mentioned two types of women entrepreneurs: "Aljapa" (who are itinerant traders) and "Alarobo" (who are described as petty traders), actually described as very prudent businesswomen. These women have started to take important political positions in their environments, thus increasing their status and positions due to the wealth gained through trading activities. Interestingly, these women entrepreneurs started micro or small businesses with minimum finances and without sufficient knowledge about new businesses. This research also shows that women develop their businesses but mostly in an informal sector with certain exceptions.

According to the United Nations Development Program (UNDP, 2004), it could be concluded that Africa has only 6% of the female workforce in high positions, like managers and executives in larger companies. In addition, 23% of women in Africa work in service branches and 5% are employed in industry. Namely, most women in Africa work in agriculture and in food production, less in nonagricultural branches. This is understandable, because there is on the one side the deficit of food in many African countries and on the other side there is woman's need to support and to help their family to survive. Accordingly, women do very hard work without specified working hours, by doing household work, selling on the market, and so on. Despite that, African women still did not gain respect in society, which they, by their work engagement, deserve.

Beside difficult working conditions, African women face another problem. According to statistical data from Addis Ababa–based Economic Commission of Africa (ECA), provide around 58% of all African women are HIV infected (Akinwumi, 2000). Despite this problem, a number of women still manage to fight for greater rights and to take part in politics in their countries. These women have demonstrated their abilities and showed that they should be seriously considered as important in the political and economic spheres in their societies. Therefore, nongovernmental organizations around the world are now creating and implementing projects to encourage entrepreneurship as a pathway out of poverty. Many programs specifically target women in Third World countries. This organization has helped dozens of low-income women start their own businesses and design them based on the principle of cooperative ownership.

GLOBALIZATION AND GENDER ROLES

Globalization has had a major impact on gender roles. Many critics fear that globalization, in the sense of integration of a country into world society, will cause gender inequality. It may harm women in several ways:

- Economically, through discrimination in favor of male workers, marginalization of women in unpaid or informal labor, exploitation of women in low-wage sweatshop settings, and/or impoverishment though loss of traditional sources of income.

- Politically, through exclusion from the domestic political process and loss of control to global pressures.
- Culturally, through loss of identity and autonomy to a hegemonic global culture.

On the other side, Janet Momsen from Kings College and the London School of Economics and Political Science stressed in her latest book, *Gender and Development* (2004), that globalization gives poor women a brighter future. Much of the benefits of globalization for women are more political and social than economic, Momsen says. She points to a growing confidence and sense of power, as poor women are able to earn more money, feed their children, and earn their husbands' respect.

Gender roles around the world varied due to many factors, and if globalization does anything to change this fact, it would be through the exchange of knowledge. New technology and the Internet have helped globalization, and we believe that it should help lessen the gap between the rich and the poor, however, not as much as it could. The Internet has allowed knowledge to spread much faster than was possible before. The knowledge allows people to take opportunities they did not have before. There is now global interaction with groups of women talking about everything from how to handle domestic violence to how to start small businesses.

In other words, it helps ideas spread through the world and allows ideas to be shared. While it does allow ideas to be shared to places across the world, it allows rich countries to spread ideas among themselves, leading to a global knowledge increase, one that helps lower the gap between the rich and the poor.

Because of globalization, there has been a growing exposure of countries around the world to foreign cultures and peoples. Thus, the most noticeable example of globalization on gender roles can be seen in those countries that give in to global example and begin to promote national equality where there was once extreme inequality.

CONCLUSION

Despite certain steps forward in developing countries in which gradually women's position have improved, they are far behind women in highly developed countries in terms of:

1. Educational level
2. Business type
3. Position hierarchy of employees, which are still dominated by men

4. Working on less-paid jobs or not paid at all
5. Working in hard conditions
6. Absence of suitable public and private modes of financing
7. They have no financial support from family or society for starting their own business in a formal economy
8. Women are faced with specific obstacles such as family responsibilities that have to be overcome in order to give them access to the same opportunities as men
9. Women still represent a minority of those that start new firms, are self-employed, or are small business owner-managers
10. Lack of role models in entrepreneurship
11. Lack of relevant networks and women's mobility

In addition, analysis showed that more and more women do not wish to completely abandon their traditional role, which they have in their families, but want to add to it by other types of engagements in which they will later be fulfilled and proved.

REFERENCES

Akinwumi, O (2000). Women entrepreneurs in Nigeria. *Africa Update Newsletter,* 7(3). Available at http://www.ccsu.edu/afstudy/upd7-3.htm

Alsos, G. A., & Ljunggren, E. (1998) Does the business start-up process differs by gender. A longitudinal study of nascent entrepreneurs. In P. D. Reynolds, W. D. Bygrave, S. Manigart, C. M. Mason, G. D. Meyer, N. M. Carter, & K. G. Shaver (Eds.), *Frontiers of entrepreneurial research* (pp. 137–151). Boston: Babson College.

Andre, R. (1992) A national profile of women's participation in networks of small business leaders. *Journal of Small Business Management, 30*(1), 66–73.

Bird, B. (1989). *Enterpreneurial behaviour.* Scott, Foresman.

Marković, M. R. (2006). *Entrepreneurship—theoretical and practical guide on all aspects for starting up small business.* Belgrade: Link Group.

Murdoch,J., (1999). The microfinance promise. *Journal of Economic Literature, 37*(4), 1596–1614.

CHAPTER 2

PAST FEMALE ENTREPRENEURSHIP WITH THE STRESS ON THE FUTURE IN NEW ECONOMY GLOBALIZATION

Maika Valencia

INTRODUCTION

The increasing presence of women in the business field as entrepreneurs or business owners in the last decades has changed the demographic characteristics of entrepreneurs. Women-owned businesses are playing a more active role in society and the economy, representing about 25.8–28% of total entrepreneurs in the world (see Table 2.1). This fact is inspiring academics, policymakers, and world institutions to focus on this interesting phenomenon. Could the increase of women in professional activities such as entrepreneurship result from social evolution in regard to gender role perception? Do sociocultural factors have a direct positive influence on the increasing presence of women in the entrepreneurial world? Are changes in institutional factors such as public economic policies conducive to female entrepreneurial activity? These are just some of the questions that

The Perspective of Women's Entrepreneurship in the Age of Globalization, pages 13–23
Copyright © 2007 by Information Age Publishing
All rights of reproduction in any form reserved.

TABLE 2.1
Evolution of Women Entrepreneurs (1970–1999)
(Percentages of women entrepreneurs over total entrepreneurs)

	1970–79	1980–89	1990–99
Australia	24.5	29.6	32.1
Belgica	25.0	26.3	27.4
Canada	25.4	30.8	37.1
Finland	43.9	36.8	33.0
Germany	43.5	32.9	27.2
Greece	32.9	18.1	20.1
Italy	27.5	22.3	23.7
Japan	30.1	31.3	30.0
South Korea	24.8	27.3	27.9
New Zealand	14.3	27.6	29.5
Norway	16.1	19.1	25.4
Spain	20.4	22.6	26.1
Sweden	16.8	26.8	25.4
United Kingdom	19.6	23.1	25.0
United States	22.1	29.7	35.2
OECD	25.8	26.4	28.2

Source: OECD (2001, p. 23).

need to be explored in order to explain the increasing presence of women as business owners.

This phenomenon has been recognized in the business and management scientific community during the 1980s, mainly in Anglo-Saxon countries. Important academic publications[1] have encouraged the creation of studies on women as business owners. Advances in this field of study have been helped by the fact that world institutions such as the United Nations and the Organization for Economic Cooperation and Development have recognized the importance of producing reports and statistics separated by gender and have encouraged their member countries to carry out such studies.

This chapter attempts to present a review of the female entrepreneurship in the world from its origins as a field of study with the stress on the future. Using the new venture creation phenomenon as the criteria to review the literature and Gartner's (1985) four-dimensional conceptual framework to make a classification of studies according to the dimensions involved in the venture creation. The individual dimension (the entrepreneur), the organization dimension (the venture created), the process dimension (previous activities to start a venture), and the environment dimension (external factors) are presented. This structure recognizes the complexity and variation that thrives in the new venture creation phenomenon.

The entrepreneur (individual dimension). In the field of entrepreneurship, the earliest studies had focused on the figure of the entrepreneur, concentrating on the sociodemographical and psychological characterization at an individual level. The female entrepreneurship field has followed the same pattern, being the individual dimension first to be studied. Empirical studies tried to identify the personal characteristics that could define and differentiate entrepreneurs from nonentrepreneurs (Fagenson, 1993; Low & MacMillan, 1988). It was believed research from these perspectives could offer significant explanatory and predictive potential about the entrepreneur.

Even though most of the articles published in the last decades are about the individual dimension, it could be said no major differences were found between male and female entrepreneurs (Brush, 1992; Catley & Hamilton, 1998). Both utilize a common entrepreneur profile, except for experience in professional activities, education in the business field, and experience in startup companies (Brush, 1992; Brush & Bird, 1996; Hisrich, Brush, Good, & DeSouza, 1997; Lamolla, 2005; Minniti, Arenius, & Langowitz, 2005).

The Global Entrepreneurship Monitor (GEM) realized in 2004 a cross-national study on women's entrepreneurial activity, the first study launched by the Consortium on Female Entrepreneurship. This study included members of 34 countries from all over the world.[2] The results related to the traits perspective were that women entrepreneurs range in ages 25–34, except in the high-income countries where it was 35–44, are married, and have children.

Within the psychological characterization studies, what motivates the entrepreneur to create a business? There are many motives for a person to become an entrepreneur. Institutions and authors have classified them as "necessity-push" and "opportunity-pull" motivations. "Push"-motivated entrepreneurs are those whose dissatisfaction with their current position, for reasons unrelated to their entrepreneurial characteristics, pushes them to start a venture. "Pull"-motivated entrepreneurs are those who are attracted by their new venture idea and initiate venture activity because of the attractiveness of the business idea and its personal implications (Amit & Muller, 1994; Bygrave, 2002; www.gemconsortium.org). Some of the main push and pull motivations for women to become entrepreneurs are (1) push factors are dissatisfaction with their job, flexibility to manage family obligations, independence, and work aspirations; and (2) pull factors are self-fulfilment, family and lifestyle motivators, and social recognition (DeMartino & Barbato, 2003; Kourilsky & Walstad, 1998; Kyro, 2001).

In the near future special attention should be paid to the most recent studies that explore a genetic basis for special attributes of women in social ability and empathy, and the role these attributes play in venture creation. The social feminism theory should be further studied to determine how the societal experience of women influences their entrepreneurial activity. These conclusions were made as a result of what have been observed in the tendency of the latest papers published, the small quantity of research dedicated to these less-explored areas, and because it would be more interesting to focus on these theories since most authors conclude women and men use common personal characteristics as entrepreneurs. So, it will be worth looking at new theories that point on new aspects of skills and personality.

The organization dimension. The research realized about organizations created by women has studied the objects of ownership, sectors of activity, management strategies, business performance, and success.

According to Rosa and Hamilton (1994), there were no significant differences between men and women entrepreneurs in forms of ownership of ventures. Some differences were found in forms of association. Men frequently form associations with four or more other owners, while women form associations with just one other owner (most likely a domestic partner). Another distinction in women's organizations is that they tend to have domestic partners and other relatives who contribute to the business in some way.

Regarding strategies created in the new venture, a general strategy followed in greater degree in women-owned businesses is a product-service quality strategy (Chaganti & Parasuraman, 1996). With respect to the rhythm of growth, women tend to have slower early growth trajectories (Minniti et al., 2005). Women showed a preference for slower-growth strategies due to the risks associated with fast-paced growth strategies (Cliff, 1998).

In relation to financing strategies, women and men entrepreneurs generally use one external source of finance—a credit bank (Hokkanen, Lumme, & Autio, 1998). Due to the characteristics of women-owned businesses and their activity sector, they are more likely consumer-oriented businesses, small companies, and are involved in traditional sectors, especially in the service sector (Anna, Chandler, Jansen, & Mero, 1999; Minniti, 2005). All these factors influence that financing strategy be very simple; providing most women with all the required start-up capital themselves. Financing through the use of venture capital in women-owned businesses is still very uncommon; very few women entrepreneurs receive equity. Those who do are women whose companies have large sales figures and whose owners have more training or expertise in finance and prior experience as senior executives (Allen & Carter, 1996; Brush, Carter, Greene, &

Hart, 2000; Carter, 2002). It is important to point out that these cases were observed in the United States, where women-owned businesses are more diversified than those in developing countries, and they are able to have access to this kind of financing.

Business performance of women entrepreneurs' companies findings can be grouped into two categories: authors who maintain that there is a similar performance in women- and men-owned organizations (Watson, 2002; Watson & Robinson, 2003), and authors who suggest women-owned organizations are lower in performance than men-owned organizations (Fischer et al., 1993; Sexton & Robinson, 1989; Srinivasan, Woo, & Cooper, 1994). As the above empirical studies cited, it can be observed the way in which performance is measured that results diverge. All these studies have in common that they make reference to performance as equivalent to an economic performance, and not considering other variables to measure such as owner's expectations, company goals, and so on. As Solymossy (1998) refers, measuring success is to some extent problematic due to an absence of consensus as to what constitutes entrepreneurial success; various success dimensions belong to economic performance, measuring only one aspect of success: economic. And there is another aspect that is frequently missed, which refers to the subjective part of the entrepreneur's expectations, which in the case of women entrepreneurs, results are very significant.

Research carried out on this dimension implies the need of further studies that could give a better understanding to the women entrepreneurs phenomenon. For instance, it would be interesting to explore the role that has personal achievement rather than economic achievement as a success indicator, or identify key variables involved in organizational strategies adequated to the type of companies created by women. Also, future studies should draw special attention to the sector or industries in which the ventures created by women are situated (Anna et al., 1999; Rosa & Hamilton, 1994), and focus on the performance measurement indicators used in women-owned businesses. Because of differences observed on performance measurement and their different conclusions, it is worth mentioning that most performance studies just consider economic elements and not deal with levels of satisfaction, which should be taken into account since women consider them very important. A very small quantity of research was dedicated to the analysis of strategic and structural forms of organizations run by women.

The Process Dimension. There are very few studies focusing on the process dimension within the female-entrepreneurship field of research. Studies involve startup activities, strategies, and organization design used for women.

In the variety of entrepreneurial activities carried out during the startup process, women entrepreneurs elaborate on business plans to a lesser extent, have a larger need for external capital, hire employees to a lesser extent, and, on the average, take more time between initiations of activities (Alsos & Ljunggren, 1998). These observations are in correspondence to what have been mentioned above in the organization dimension, regarding the type of business created by women (e.g., involved in traditional sectors, small business size, etc.), because of their business characteristics it is not necessary for large external capital or to hire employees, and so on.

Startup activities play a critical role in both the survival and growth of a business, Alsos and Ljunggren (1998) state there were similar success rates for men and women in setting up a business even though their startup activities had differences. But Srinivasan (2004) suggests that maybe these differences are the determining factors in why women-owned businesses present lower rates of survival and growth than men-owned businesses. Taking into account the kind of women-owned companies, mostly micro and small businesses, we considered that the manner of how the venture-creation process is completed is vital for their survival.

The process of how men and women entrepreneurs organize their businesses seems similar. Both prefer to start a business with someone they know well or have had ties with on a social level, and both prefer same-sex teams. Social networking and social capital play an important role for women entrepreneurs (Aldrich, Carter, & Ruef, 2002).

The new venture creation process is the least explored within the female entrepreneurship literature. Therefore, several topics under this field need to be explored in order to identify the critical variables presented in the venture creation process as well as specific activities women engage in to create a new business, giving special attention to networking theory and social capital roles.

The environment dimension. Entrepreneurship is generally accepted to be a contextual phenomenon, affected by the economic, political, social, and cultural environment in which it occurs (Lumpkin & Dess, 1996; Steams & Hills, 1996; cited in Solymossy, 1998). In the female entrepreneurship field, literature reviewed under this dimension has focused mostly on issues referring to accessibility and availability of capital through debt financing, from a perspective of gender discrimination. We cannot find any studies that focus on other variables influencing venture creation by women entrepreneurs.

The economic theory formulated by North (1990), institutional economy, utilized in studies in the entrepreneurship field is useful to give an order to empirical studies, classifying them into "formal institutions" and "informal institutions," the former term referring to all legal frames and the latter referring to sociocultural values within the society. Taking this into account it could be said that most of the empirical studies reviewed are focused on the formal institutions (e.g., capital access, regulations, etc.) and very few others focused on the "informal institutions" (e.g., attitudes and perceptions of society, family support, etc.).

In formal institutions, mixed results were found concerning external debt financing such as bank loans. Several studies state that there was no proof of discrimination against women on the basis of gender in terms of access to capital and terms of credit (loan size, interest rate, or interest margin). Lenders mainly discriminate on the basis of business size, preferring to lend to larger businesses and women-owned businesses, which, in most of the cases, are smaller than men-owned businesses (Coleman, 1998; Fabowale, Orser, & Riding, 1995; Hokkanen et al., 1998; Read, 1994). Here again, it is important to point out that all the empirical studies cited above make reference to samples in developed countries and therefore differ from the situation found in developing countries. In the case of developing countries, inaccessibility to external financing for women is notorious. The existence of special financing programs for women through development banks or women's associations (i.e., the Women's World Bank) are examples that the necessity exists and that market institutions are not fulfilling it. Even in developed countries, women perceive difficulties in access to financing. According to Coleman (1998) and Fay and Williams (1993), women may experience gender discrimination when seeking startup capital and with the terms of credit, but that a high level of education and a good relationship with the financial institution may help them compensate for this disadvantage.

The most recent studies on capital access explore the equity-financing market for women-owned companies. These studies has been realized in the United States, Greene, Brush, Hart, and Saparito (1999) point out that a very small percentage of women-owned businesses have access to these resources. It is important to note that very few women-owned businesses are in the high-growing sectors, which are the ones characterized in this kind of lending market. They explain that the institutional environment of the venture capital industry is a close and tightly interconnected network. Women, by extension of the social network theory, are left out of this formal venture capital network.

In informal institutions, social networking has played a very important role in the field of entrepreneurship and venture creation. As the GEM explored in their study on women entrepreneurs, mentoring and network support are crucial in boosting women's attitudes with respect to leadership and new venture creation. Aldrich (1989), and Moore and Buttner (1997) mention that men and women create different types of networks, and that women's networks are characterized by having more informal associations and by having same-gender members.

Other variables explored within cultural aspects refer to perception of entrepreneurship, family environment, and formal employment barriers. A study by Holmquist (2001) is one of the few studies analyzing the role of sociocultural variables. A cross-country comparative analysis between the United States and Sweden was carried out, analyzing cultural aspects related to the presence of women in entrepreneurship. Holmquist sustains that there are culturally based differences in perceptions of entrepreneurship and gender roles. Her research proves that the distance between being an entrepreneur and an employee and between male and female roles were different for each context analyzed.

Other studies confirm the view that social attitudes toward women in business have an impact on women's aspirations toward business creation. Family support is crucial in the business setup, especially in developing countries, as was observed in several empirical researches. Huq and Richardson (1997) ran an empirical study to explore the issues surrounding the aspiration of a woman to set up her own business in a developing country (Bangladesh); findings showed family support is a critical factor. Glas and Petrin (1998) found family support was an important variable involved in entrepreneurial career choices of women in Slovenia. Shabbir and Di Gregorio (1996) realized a study in Pakistan exploring how women interpret structural factors that influence the process of business startups; and women expressed that for them that was essential to have internal resources (e.g., qualifications, experience) and family support in order to start a business.

It is well stated in all the studies mentioned above that social attitude to female entrepreneurship plays a critical role. Other formal structures, such as the formal employment market and corporative world, affecting women's decisions to start their own businesses due to the "glass ceiling" issue (Alvarez & Meyer, 1998). These two areas identified influence women's decision to become entrepreneurs; we consider that cross-country studies would be helpful to contrast how these factors affect women in developing and developed countries.

CONCLUSION

Female entrepreneurship is having a greater importance within economies; the GEM estimates that about 73 million people are active entrepreneurs in 34 nations, of those 40.54% are women. Female entrepreneurship can be considered a very broad and recent field of study, where several theories can be linked to the study of this phenomenon, such as gender theories, managerial theories, public policy, and so on. In this chapter we state trends emerging from the findings of previous studies on women's presence in entrepreneurial activity and future research questions and implications were discussed.

NOTES

1. Such as *Frontiers of Entrepreneurship* (Babson conference proceedings, 1981–), *Journal of Business Venturing* (1985–), and *Entrepreneurship, Theory and Practice* (formerly *American Journal of Small Business*, 1988–).

2. In order to present the results of the study, the GEM grouped the countries in three levels according to their GDP per capita: low-income, middle-income, and high-income countries. Levels were determined as follows: not exceeding US$10,000, between US$10,000 and US$25,000, and exceeding US$25,000 respectively. Low-income countries: Argentina, Brazil, Croatia, Ecuador, Hungary, Jordan, Peru, Poland, South Africa, and Uganda. Middle-income countries: Grecia, Hong Kong, Israel, New Zealand, Portugal, Singapore, Slovenia, and Spain. High-income countries: Australia, Belgium, Canada, Denmark, Finland, France, Germany, Iceland, Italy, Ireland, Japan, Netherlands, Norway, Sweden, United Kingdom, and the United States (Minniti et al., 2005).

REFERENCES

Aldrich, H. (1989). Networking among women entrepreneurs. In O. Hagan, C. Rivchun, & D. Sexton (Eds.), *Women-owned business* (pp. 103–132). New York: Praeger.

Aldrich, H., Carter, N., & Ruef, M. (2002). With very little help from their friends: Gender and relational composition of nascent entrepreneurs' start-up teams. *Frontiers of Entrepreneurship*, Babson College.

Allen, K., & Carter, N. (1996). Women entrepreneurs: Profile differences across high and low performing adolescent firms. *Frontiers of Entrepreneurship*, Babson College.

Alsos, G., & Ljunggren, E. (1998). Does the business start-up process differ by gender?: A longitudinal study of nascent entrepreneurs. *Frontiers of Entrepreneurship*, Babson College.

Alvarez, S., & Meyer, D. (1998). Why do women become entrepreneurs? *Frontiers of Entrepreneurship*, Babson College.

Amit, R., & Muller, E. (1994). "Push" and "pull" entrepreneurship. *Frontiers of Entrepreneurship*, Babson College.

Anna, A. L., Chandler, G. N., Jansen, E., & Mero, N. P. (1999). Women business owners in traditional and non-traditional industries. *Journal of Business Venturing, 15*(3), 279–303.

Brush, C. (1992). Research on women business owners: Past trends, a new perspective and future directions. *Entrepreneurship Theory and Practice*, pp. 5–30.

Brush, C., & Bird, B. (1996). Leadership vision of successful women entrepreneurs: Dimensions and characteristics. *Frontiers of Entrepreneurship*, Babson College.

Brush, C., Carter, N., Greene, P., & Hart, M. (2000). Women and equity capital: An exploration of factors affecting capital access. *Frontiers of Entrepreneurship*, Babson College.

Bygrave, W. D. (2005). *Financing entrepreneurial ventures. Global entrepreneurship monitor financing report*. Babson College and London Business School.

Carter, N. (2002). The role of risk orientation on financing expectations in new venture creation: Does sex matter? *Frontiers of Entrepreneurship*, Babson College.

Catley, S., & Hamilton, R. (1998). Small business development and gender of owner. *Journal of Management Development, 17*(1), 75–82.

Chaganti, R., & Parasuraman, S. (1996). A study of the impacts of gender on business performance and management patterns in small businesses. *Entrepreneurship Theory and Practice*, pp. 73–75.

Cliff, J. E. (1998). Does one size fit all?: Exploring the relationship between attitudes towards growth, gender, and business size. *Journal of Business Venturing, 13*(6), 523–542.

Coleman, S. (1998). Access to capital: A comparison of men and women-owned small business. *Frontiers of Entrepreneurship*, Babson College.

DeMartino, R., & Barbato, R. (2003). Differences between women and men MBA entrepreneurs: Exploring family flexibility and wealth creation as career motivators. *Journal of Business Venturing, 18*(6), 815–832.

Fabowale, L., Orser, B., & Riding, A. (1995). Gender, structural factors, and credit terms between Canadian small businesses and financial institutions. *Entrepreneurship Theory and Practice*, pp. 41–65.

Fagenson, E. A. (1993). Personal value systems of men and women entrepreneurs versus managers. *Journal of Business Venturing, 8*(5), 409–430.

Fay, M., & Williams, L. (1993). Gender bias and the availability of business loans. *Journal of Business Venturing, 8*(4), 363–376.

Fischer, E., Reuber, A. R., & Dyke, L. (1993). A theoretical overview and extension of research on sex, gender, and entrepreneurship. *Journal of Business Venturing, 8*(2), 151–168.

Gartner, W. (1985). A conceptual framework for describing the phenomenon of new venture creation. *Academy of Management Review, 10*(4), 696–706.

Glas, M., & Petrin, T. (1998). Entrepreneurship: New challenge for Slovene women. *Frontiers of Entrepreneurship*, Babson College.

Greene, P., Brush, C., Hart, M., & Saparito, P. (1999). Exploration of the venture capital industry: Is gender an issue? *Frontiers of Entrepreneurship*, Babson College.

Hisrich, R., Brush, C., Good, D., & DeSouza, G. (1997). Performance in entrepreneurial ventures: Does gender matter? *Frontiers of Entrepreneurship*, Babson College.

Hokkanen, P., Lumme, A., & Autio, E. (1998). Gender-based non-differences in bank shopping and credit terms. *Frontiers of Entrepreneurship*, Babson College.

Holmquist, C. (2001). Does culture matter for the formation of views on entrepreneurship and gender roles? Case studies of women as high-tech (IT) entrepreneurs in Boston and Stockholm. *Frontiers of Entrepreneurship*, Babson College.

Huq, A., & Richardson, P. (1997). Business ownership as an economic option for middle-income educated urban women in Bangladesh. *Frontiers of Entrepreneurship*, Babson College.

Kourilsky, M. L., & Walstad, W. B. (1998). Entrepreneurship and female youth: Knowledge, attitudes, gender differences, and educational practices. *Journal of Business Venturing, 13*(1), 77–88.

Kyro, P. (2001). Women entrepreneurs question men's criteria for success. *Frontiers of Entrepreneurship*, Babson College.

Lamolla, L. (2005). Emprender en femenino: la evolución de las políticas económicas locales para emprendedoras en Cataluña. Doctoral thesis, Universidad Autonoma de Barcelona.

Low, M., & MacMillan, I. (1988). Entrepreneurship: Past research and future challenges. *Journal of Management*, pp. 139–161.

Minniti, M., Arenius, P., & Langowitz, N. (2005). *2004 Report on Women and Entrepreneurship*. GEM.

Moore, D. P., & Buttner, E. H. (1997). *Women entrepreneurs: Moving beyond the glass ceiling*. Thousands Oaks, CA: Sage.

North, D. C. (1990). *Institutions, institutional change and economic performance*. Cambridge, UK: Cambridge University Press.

OECD (2001). Retreived from http://www.cipe.org/pdf/programs/women/jalbert .pdf.

Read, L. (1994). Raising finance from banks: A comparative study of the experiences of male and female business owners. *Frontiers of Entrepreneurship*, Babson College.

Rosa, P., & Hamilton, D. (1994). Gender and ownership in UK small firms. *Entrepreneurship Theory and Practice*, pp. 11–27.

Sexton, E. A., & Robinson, P. B. (1989). The Economic and Demographic Determinants of Self-Employment. *Frontiers of Entrepreneurship*, Babson College.

Shabbir, A., & Di Gregorio, S. (1996). An examination of the relationship between women's personal goals and structural factors influencing their decision to start a business: The case of Pakistan. *Journal of Business Venturing, 11*(6), 507–529.

Solymossy, E. (1998). *Entrepreneurial dimensions: the relationship of individual, venture, and environmental factors to success*. Doctoral dissertation, Case Western Reserve University.

Srinivasan, R., Woo, C., & Cooper, A. (1994). Performance determinants for male and female entrepreneurs. *Frontiers of Entrepreneurship*, Babson College.

Watson, J. (2002). Comparing the performance of male- and female-controlled businesses: Relating outputs to inputs. *Entrepreneurship Theory and Practice*, pp. 91–100.

Watson, J., & Robinson, S. (2003). Adjusting for risk in comparing the performances of male- and female-controlled SMEs. *Journal of Business Venturing, 18*(6), 773–788.

CHAPTER 3

CULTIVATING ENTREPRENEURSHIP AMONG WOMEN IN THE 21ST CENTURY

Olugbenga Adesanya

INTRODUCTION

Our female folks must cultivate the entrepreneurship spirit. Some 500 million persons worldwide were either actively involved in trying to start a new venture or were owner-managers of a new business in 2005. Entrepreneurs are driving a revolution that is transforming and renewing economics worldwide. There, however, exists the need for increased female participation and renewed economics worldwide. Entrepreneurship is the basis of free enterprise since the growing of new businesses gives vitality to a market economy. New and emerging businesses bring up a large proportion of new products and services that influence the way we work and live, such as personal computers, software, the Internet, biotechnology, beauty product, drugs, hospitality services, and cottage industrial goods. They generate most of the new jobs.

The Perspective of Women's Entrepreneurship in the Age of Globalization, pages 25–37
Copyright © 2007 by Information Age Publishing
All rights of reproduction in any form reserved.

UNDERSTANDING THE E-PROCESS

The 21st century is a good time to encourage the imbibing of the art and science of entrepreneurship among women for empowerment. But what is entrepreneurship? Early this century, Joseph Schumpeter, the Moravian-born economist writing in Vienna, gave us the modern definition of an entrepreneur as the person who destroys the existing economic order by promoting new approaches and new products and services, and by exploiting new raw materials. According to Schumpeter, that person is most likely to accomplish this destruction by founding a new business but may also do it within an existing one.

Women must be doubly prepared and have cutting-edge ideas to equal the feat of Mary Kay, for example The *Portable MBA in Entrepreneurship* defines it as one who starts a new and potentially successful business. An entrepreneur is a person who perceives an opportunity and creates an organization to pursue it. Women should strive to understand the entrepreneurial process as it concerns issues and actions relating to dreaming dreams and creating systems to realize them. Women entrepreneurs' new businesses may, in a few cases, be the revolutionary sort that rearranges the global economic order, such as Wal-Mart, FedEx, Microsoft, Mary Kay, and Expedia.com, are now doing. The key is for the weaker sex to have the mentality of wealth creation even on an incremental basis.

POSERS

Should the birthing of a new business be subjected to luck or probability chance? Should the art and science of entrepreneurship be taught to women? The answer is yes. Women should be taught since entrepreneurship represents a fast track to overcoming poverty by the female folks in tertiary institutions "globally."

The resulting education and upgrading through specialized education and the attendant entrepreneurial change due to the body of knowledge on entrepreneurship should be developed and reviewed every 5 years to flow with trends and blend with prevailing cultures. The process of creating a new business is well understood by everyone, especially women who bear the burden of financial lack in the average household. The objective should not be to produce a Bill Gates or a Donna Karan. It is time to turn women into creative students with nuggets to start a business, and the world will end up with better entrepreneurs.

NEW ENTERPRISE STARTUP KIT

Let us start by analyzing the entrepreneurial flow, that is, the in-dwelling, social, and environmental factors that give rise to a new enterprise. A person gets an idea for a new business either through a deliberate search or through an unexpected encounter. The decision to pursue that idea to function depends on factors such as alternative career prospects, family, friends, role models, the state of the economy, and the availability of resources both fiscal and human.

Melanie Stevens was a high school dropout who, after a number of minor jobs, had little or no career options. She decided to make canvas bags to make a living. She met with success as a chain of retail stores was built throughout Canada. A few years later, talking of disappointments, Howard Rose had been laid off four times as a result of merges and consolidations in the pharmaceutical firm, and decided to start his own drug packaging company, Waverly Pharmaceutical. Tim Waterstone founded Waterstone's Bookstores after W.H. Smith fired him. A UK bus industry deregulation made Ann Gloag quit her nursing job and invest her bus driver father's $40,000 severance pay to set up a bus company, Stagecoach, with her brother.

For other people, entrepreneurship is a deliberate career choice. Sandra Kurtzig was a software engineer with General Electric who wanted to start a family and work at home. She started ASKd Computer System Inc., which became a $400 million annual business. Women are encouraged to ape Sandra and make headway.

Where is the source of ideas for prospective entrepreneurs? A 2002 study of the Inc. 500—comprising America's [500] fastest-growing companies—found that 57% of the founders got the idea for their new venture in the industry they worked in and a further 23% in an industry related to the one in which they were employed. As a result, 80% of all new high-success businesses are established in economic sectors that are close to familiar investments. The learning curve starts with previous or present job experiences. Serial or repeated efforts, like that of Crugnale, is instructive. He, as an Inc. 500 Hall of fame honoree, became a partner at Steve's Ice Cream, and established a 26-unit national franchise. Some time in 1982, Crugnale started Bertucci's where gourmet pizza was cooked in wood-fired brick ovens and built it into a nationwide chain of 90 restaurants. Naked Restaurants was introduced as an incubator to develop his innovative dining concepts. The first one, the Naked Fish, opened in 1999 and brought his wood fired grill approach to a new niche: fresh fish and meats with a touch of Cubanismo. The second restaurant, Red Sauce, followed in 2002, serving cheaper authentic Italian food close to the lines of Bertucci's.

In 1981, James Clark, a Stanford University computer science professor, founded Silicon Graphics, a computer manufacturer with 1996 sales of $3 billion. In April 1994, he teamed up with Marc Andreessen to found Netscape Communications. Within 12 months, its browser software, Navigator, dominated the Internet's World Wide Web. By August 1995, when Netscape was quoted, Clark emerged the first Internet billionaire. Almost a year later in June 1996, Clark promoted another firm, Healthcare, to assist doctors, insurers, and patients to exchange information and engage in Internet-based businesses using Netscape's Navigator software.

THE NINE Ds

Dreaming. Entrepreneurs should have a vision of what they desire to do to create wealth. It is essential that they should either have the ability to implement their dreams, or train to acquire the skills and temperaments of business-minded people.

Decide fast. Do not procrastinate. Make decisions swiftly. Swiftness is a key factor in success.

Doers. Be a doer. Decide on a course of action, and implement it as quickly as possible.

Determination. Be determined to implement the ventures with your everything you have.

Dedication. Be totally dedicated to the idea turning into a business proposal. This could be at a heavy cost to relationships with colleagues, friends, and family members, especially the husbands and children of female entrepreneurs. Travail tirelessly.

Devotion. As a business woman, you should love what you do. It is love that sustains the venture when the going gets tough. And it is love of their product or service that makes them so effective at selling it.

Details. In starting and growing a business, the entrepreneur must be on top of the critical details.

Destiny. Have your destiny in your hands; depend on articulation.

Distribute. Entrepreneurs distribute the ownership of their business with key workers who are critical to the success of the business. Share the burden and see the gains.

ENVIRONMENTAL FACTORS

Perhaps as important as personal attributes are the external influences on a would-be entrepreneur. It's no accident that some parts of the world are more entrepreneurial than others. The most famous region of high-tech entrepreneurship is Silicon Valley. Because everyone in Silicon Valley knows someone who has made it big as an entrepreneur, role models abound. This situation produces what Stanford University sociologist Everett Rogers called "Silicon Valley fever." It seems as if everyone in the valley catches that bug sooner or later and wants to start a business. There are venture capitalists who understand how to select and nurture high-tech entrepreneurs, bankers who specialize in lending to them, lawyers who understand the importance of intellectual property and how to protect it, landlords who are experienced in renting real estate to fledgling companies, suppliers who are willing to sell goods on credit to companies with no credit history, and even politicians who are supportive.

Role models are very important because knowing a successful entrepreneur makes the act of becoming one seem much more credible.

Would-be entrepreneurs come into contact with role models primarily in the home and at work. If you have a close relative who is an entrepreneur, it is more likely that you will have a desire to become an entrepreneur; it is especially true if that relative is your mother or father. At Babson College, more than half of the undergraduates studying entrepreneurship come from families that own businesses. But you don't have to be from a business-owning family to become an entrepreneur. Bill Gates, for example, was following the family tradition of becoming a lawyer when he dropped out of Harvard and founded Microsoft. He was in the fledgling microcomputer industry, which was being built by entrepreneurs. The United States has an abundance of high-tech entrepreneurs who are household names. One of them, Ross Perot, was so well known that he became a presidential candidate, preferred by one in five American voters, in 1992.

Some universities are hotbeds of entrepreneurship. For example, the Massachusetts Institute of Technology has produced numerous entrepreneurs among its faculty and alums. Companies with an MIT connection transformed the Massachusetts economy from one based on decaying shoe and textile industries into one based on high technology. According to a 1997 study by the Bank of Boston, 125,000 jobs in Massachusetts were MIT related (Bygrave & Hofer, 1991). Nationwide in 1996, 733,000 people working in more than 8,500 plants and offices held jobs that originated with companies founded by MIT graduates. The 4,000 or so firms that MIT graduates founded accounted for at least 1.1 million jobs worldwide and generated $232 billion in revenues. If MIT-related companies were a nation, it would be the 24th largest economy in the world. The neighborhood of East Cambridge adjacent to MIT has been called "The Most Entrepreneurial Place on Earth" by *Inc.* magazine. According to *Inc.,* roughly 10% of Massachusetts software companies and approximately 20% of the state's 280 biotechnology companies are headquartered in that square mile.

- It is not only in high-tech that half of all the convenience stores in New York City are owned by Koreans.
- It was the visibility of successful role models that spread catfish farming in the Mississippi Delta as a more profitable alternative to cotton.
- The *Pacific Northwest* has more microbreweries *than any other region of* the United States.
- In the vicinity of the town of Wells, Maine, are half a dozen second-hand bookstores.

African Americans make up 12% of the U.S. population, but owned only 4% of the nation's businesses in 1997 (Cooper, Woo, & Dunkelberg, 1988). One of the major reasons for a relative lack of entrepreneurship among Africa Americans is the scarcity of African American entrepreneurs, especially storeowners, to provide role models. A similar problem exists among Native Americans. Lack of credible role models is also one of the big challenges in the formerly Communist European nations as they strive to become entrepreneurial.

SOCIOLOGICAL FACTORS

In addition to role models, entrepreneurs are influenced by sociological factors. *Family responsibilities* play in important role in deciding to start a company. It is, relatively speaking, an easy career decision to start a business when a person is 25 years old, single, and without many personal assets and dependents. It is a much harder decision when a person is age 45 and married, has teenage children preparing to go to college, a hefty mortgage, car payments, and a secure, well-paying job. A 1992 survey of European high-potential entrepreneurs, for instance, found that on average they had 50% of their net worth tied up in their businesses. And at 45-plus years old, if you fail as an entrepreneur, it is not easy to rebuild a career working for another company. But despite the risks, plenty of 45-year-olds are taking the plunge; in fact, the median age of the CEOs of the 500 fastest growing small companies, according to *Inc. 500* in 2000, was 40. The risks are there; all you need as a mature person is a clear mind and the zeal to be successful.

In addition, a factor that determines the age at which entrepreneurs start businesses is the balancing between the *experience that* comes with age and the *optimism* and *energy* of youth. Over time people gain experience, but sometimes too much knowledge of the industry makes businesspeople pessimistic about the chance of succeeding in new sole businesses you decide to go out on your own. Someone who has just enough experience to feel confident as a manager is more likely to feel optimistic about an entrepreneurial career. Maybe the ideal combination is a beginner's mind with the experience of an industry veteran. A beginner's mind looks at situations from a new perspective, with an exploratory spirit.

At 27 years old, Robert Swanson had the idea that a firm could be formed to capitalize on biotechnology. At that time, he knew almost nothing about the field. By reading the scientific literature, Swanson identified the leading biotechnology scientists and contacted them. "Everyone I talked to said I was too early—it would take 10 years to turn out the first microorganism from a human hormone or maybe 20 years to have a commercial product—everybody except Herb Boyer." Swanson was referring to Professor Herbet Boyer at the University of California at San Francisco, coinventor of the patent that, according to some observers, forms the basis of the biotechnology industry. Partners joined in an endeavor to explore the commercial possibilities of recombinant DNA. Boyer named their venture Genentech and announced its first success, a genetically engineered human brain hormone, somatosin. According to Swanson, they accomplished 10 years of development in 7 months (i.e., under a fiscal year). Obviously, adherence to the nine d's can make impossibility realizable within a short time. Why don't you make an attempt this season and empower yourself in the highly improbable areas of business?

Marc Andressen had a beginner's mind that produced a vision for the Internet that until then had eluded many computer industry veterans, including Bill Gates. When Andressen's youthful creativity was joined with James Clark's entrepreneurial wisdom, earned from a dozen or so years as founder and chairperson of Silicon Graphics, it turned out to be an awesome combination. Their company, Netscape, distributed 38 million copies of Navigator in just 2 years, making it the most successful new software introduction ever.

Before leaving secure, well-paying, satisfying jobs, would-be entrepreneurs should make a careful estimate of how much *sales revenue* their new business must generate before they will be able to match the income that they presently earn. It usually comes as quite a shock when they realize that at least $600,000 is needed to pay themselves a salary of $70,000 plus fringe benefits such as health care coverage, retirement pension benefits, long-term disability insurance, vacation pay, sick leave, and perhaps subsidized meals, day-care, and education benefits. Six hundred thousand dollars a year is about $12,000 per week, or about $2,000 per day, or about $200 per hour, or $3 per minute if they are open 6 days a week, 10 hours a day. Also they will be working much longer hours and bearing much more responsibility if they become self-employed. A sure way to test the strength of a marriage is to start a company that is the sole means of support for your family.

About, 22.5% of the CEOs of the *top 500* got divorced while growing their businesses. On a brighter note, 59.2% got married and 18.3% of divorced CEOs remarried (Diochon, Gasses, Menzies, & Garand, 2001).

When they actually start a business, entrepreneurs need a host of *contacts,* including customers, suppliers, investors, bankers, accountants, and lawyers. So it is important to understand where to find help before embarking on a new venture. A network of friends and business associates can be of immeasurable help in building the contacts an entrepreneur will need. They can also provide human contact because opening a business can be a lonely experience for anyone who has worked in an organization with many fellow employees.

Fortunately, today there are more organizations than ever before to help fledging entrepreneurs. Often that help is free or costs very little. The Small Business Administration (SBA) has Small Business Development Centers in every state; it funds Small Business Institutes and its Service Core of Retired Executives provides help. Some are particularly good at writing business plans, usually at no charge to the entrepreneur. There are hundreds of incubators in the United States where fledging businesses can rent space, usually at a very reasonable price, and spread some of their overhead by sharing facilities such as copying and fax machines, secretarial help, answering services, and so on. Incubators are often associated with universities, which provide free or inexpensive counseling. There are numerous associations where entrepreneurs can meet and exchange ideas.

NEW BUSINESS ANALYSIS

Having identified and defined the area to exploit, the entrepreneur should subject the idea to a thorough analysis, especially on payback period, and the internal rate of return (IRR). The banks and financial institutions and even individuals look for these indicators, coupled with the integrity of the management team, before sanction is given. Most new businesses just fade away: they are started as part-time pursuits and were never intended to become full-time businesses. Some are sold. Others are liquidated. Only 700,000 of the 2 million are legally registered as corporations or a partnership, which is a sure sign that many of the remaining 1.3 million never intended to grow. Hence, the odds that your new business will survive may not be as long as they first appear to be. If you intend to start a full-time, incorporated business, the odds that the business will survive at least 8 years with you as the owner are better than one in four; and the odds of its surviving at least 8 years a new owner are another one in four. So the 8-year survival rate for incorporated startups is about 50%.

But survival may not spell success. Too many entrepreneurs find that they can neither earn a satisfactory living in their businesses nor get out of them easily because they have too much of their personal assets tied up in them. The happiest day in an entrepreneur's life is the day doors are opened for business. For unsuccessful entrepreneurs, an even happier day may be the business is sold, especially if most personal assets remain intact. What George Bernard Shaw said about a love affair is also apt for business. Any fool can start one; it takes a genius to end one successfully.

How can you stack the odds in your family favor, so that your new business is successful? Professional investors, such as venture capitalists, have a talent for picking winners. True, they also pick losers, but a startup company funded by venture capital has, on average, a four in five chance of surviving 5 years—better odds than for the population of startup companies as a whole. Very few startup businesses—perhaps no more than one in a thousand—will ever be suitable candidates for investments from professional venture capitalists. But would-be entrepreneurs can learn much by following the evaluation process used by professional investors.

There are three crucial components for a successful new business: the opportunity, the entrepreneur (and the management team, if it's a high-potential venture), and the resources needed to start the company and make it grow.

INVESTMENT FRAMEWORK

At the center of the framework is a business plan, in which the three basic components are integrated into a complete strategic plan for the new business. The parts must fit together well. There is no point in having a first-rate idea for a new business if you have a second-rate management team. Nor are ideas and management any good without the appropriate resources.

The crucial driving force of any new venture is the lead entrepreneur and the funding management team. Georges Doriot, the founder of modern venture capital, used to say something like this: "Always consider investing in a grade A man with a grade B idea. Never invest in a grade B man with a grade A idea." He knew what he was talking about. Over the years, he invested in about 150 companies, including Digital Equipment Corporation (DEC), and watched over them as they struggled to grow. But Doriot made this statement about business in the 1950s and 1960s. During that period, there were far fewer startups each year; U.S. firms dominated the marketplace; markets were growing quickly; there was almost no competition from overseas; and most entrepreneurs were male. Today, in the global marketplace with ever-shortening product life cycles and low growth or even no growth for some of the world's leading industrial nations, the crucial ingredients for entrepreneurial success are a superb entrepreneur with a first-rate management team and an excellent market opportunity.

Women and indeed men alike should know there are three main issues for entrepreneurial success. These include a well-prepared entrepreneur backed with a first-rate management team and an excellent market opportunity.

Oftentimes people claim that success in entrepreneurship is mainly an issue of luck. There is no more luck in becoming successful at entrepreneurship than in becoming successful at anything else. In entrepreneurship, it is a question of recognizing a good opportunity when you see one and having one and having the skills to convert that opportunity into a driving business. To do that, you must be prepared. So in entrepreneurship, just like any other profession, *luck is where preparation and opportunity meet.*

In 1982 Rod Canion began Compaq to make personal computers, in spite of many big and successful competitors, including IBM and Apple. By then literally hundreds of companies were considering entering the market or had already done so. For instance, in the same week of May 1982 that DEC announced its ill-fated personal computer, four other companies introduced PCs. Despite the competition, Ben Rosen of the venture capital firm Sevin Rosen Management Company invested in Compaq. Started initially to make transportable PCs, it quickly added a complete range of high-performance PCs and grew so fast that it soon broke Apple's record for the fastest time from founding to listing on the *Fortune* 500.

Ben Rosen the venture capitalist saw in the Compaq proposal what it takes to make it stand out from all the other personal computer startups. The difference was Rod Canion and his team. Rod Canion had earned a reputation as an excellent manager at Texas Instruments. Furthermore, the market for personal computers topped $5 billion and was growing at a torrid pace. So Rosen found a superb team with a product targeted at an undeveloped niche—transportable PCs—in a large market that was growing explosively. By 1994, Compaq was the leading PC manufacturer, with 13% of the market. The catch phrase is "transportable PC." Refuse to replicate the achievements of other people; carve a niche for yourself. Think it out and get on to the ladder of success your, gender not withstanding.

LEARN FROM OTHERS SUCCESS NUGGETS

Time is life. To waste your time is to waste your life.

—Merrill Douglass

Self-Discipline

Success is nothing more than a few simple disciplines practiced daily, while failure is simply a few errors in judgment, repeated on a daily basis. The accumulative weight of our discipline and judgment leads us to either fortune or failure.

—Jim Rohn

Poverty and riches often change places, the former comes through well-conceived and carefully executed plans. Poverty needs no plans, as it is bold and worthless. Attract riches for they are shy and timid.

—Napoleon Hill

Have Direction in Life

It does not matter so much where we stand as the direction in which we head.

—Oliver Wendel

Have a Saving Culture

Enduring financial fortune is built on a foundation of saving. No short cut; no bye-pass. Show me a self-made millionaire and I will show you a dedicated savor.

—M. Leboeuf

Information is Power

Earlier on, wealth was measured in land, gold, oil and machines. Today, principal measure of wealth is information—its quality, quantity and the speed with which we require it and adept it.

—Bill Clinton

Have Faith

Continue to see the light at the end of the tunnel—I mean the thriving business. Exercise your faith.

—Gbenga Adesanya

Uphold Integrity

Ability in any form which is not counter balanced by honesty of purpose and sound character may become a tool for evil instead of good.

—Napoleon Hill

Apply Principle Strictly

Riches are to be found not in knowing the principles, but in the clear, strong and definitive application of those principles.

—Brian Sher

Diversify your Investment

Take responsibility for your finances or take orders all your life. You're either a master of money or a slave to it.

—Robert Kiyosaki

Take Charge

You must take personal responsibility. You cannot change the circumstances, the seasons or the wind, but you can change yourself.

—Jim Rohn

You can never have true freedom without financial freedom.

—Robert Kiyosaki

Think It Out Positively

Your mental attitude determines your wealth altitude.

—Gbenga Adesanya

Add to Definition of Entrepreneur

To essence of business is the ability to offer a product or service that people will pay for at a given and sufficient price above the cost of production.

—Brian Tracy

Habit is Vital

The individual who wants to reach the top in business must appreciate the might of force of habit and must understand that practices are what create habits. He must be quick to break those habits that can break her and hasten to adopt those that will become the habits that help to achieve the desired success.

—J. Paul Getty

REFERENCES

Ajzen, I. (1991). The theory of planned behavior. *Organizational Behavior and Human Decision Processes, 50,* 179–211.

Bygrave, W. D., & Hofer, C. W. (1991). Theorizing about entrepreneurship. *Entrepreneurship Theory and Practice, 16*(2), 13–22.

Cooper, A., Woo, C., & Dunkelberg, W. (1988). Entrepreneurs' perceived chances for success. *Journal of Business Venturing, 3,* 97–108.

Delmar, F., & Davidsson, P. (2000). Where do they come from?: Prevalence and characteristics of nascent entrepreneurs. *Entrepreneurship and Regional Development, 12,* 1–23.

Diochon, M., Gasses, Y., Menzies, T., & Garand, D. (2001). From conception to inception: Initial findings from the Canadian Study on entrepreneurial emergence. *Administrative Science of Canada Conference Proceedings, 22,* 41–51.

Forbes, D. P. (1999). Cognitive approaches to new venture creation. *International Journal of Management Reviews, 1*(4), 415–439.

PART II

WOMEN ENTREPRENEURS, MANAGERS, AND LEADERS

Challenges and Opportunities in Developed, Developing, and Transitional Economies

CHAPTER 4

LA VITA IMPRENDITORIALE

Female and Male Entrepreneurs in Italy

Siri Terjesen and Vanessa Ratten

INTRODUCTION

Female entrepreneurship is growing (OECD, 2000), with some estimates that this growth exceeds that of most economies around the world (Carter & Williams, 2005). In a forty-one country study, females comprise 36% of all entrepreneurs (Reynolds, Bygrave, & Autio, 2004), with the percentage of female entrepreneurs ranging from 2% in Japan to 18% in Thailand (Minniti, Arenius, & Langowitz, 2006).

To start their businesses, entrepreneurs must be able to access resources, such as customers, suppliers, market information, and financial capital. Entrepreneurs often turn to their own financial resources, and also those available from friends, family, and foolhardy investors. This study includes both male and female entrepreneurs and explores sex differences.

This research answers calls for studies of gender and entrepreneurship (Bird & Brush, 2002; Brush, 1992) and the supply and demand of entrepreneurial finance (Carter, Brush, Greene, Gatewood, & Hart, 2003; Greene, Gatewood, Brush, & Carter, 2004). The chapter is organized as follows. First, we provide an overview of the Italian national context and the

The Perspective of Women's Entrepreneurship in the Age of Globalization, pages 41–53

41

historical role of women's involvement in the labor force and in self-employment. Next, we provide a brief overview of research at the individual entrepreneur level, focusing on demographics and personal context. Four hypotheses are put forward. Next, we turn to the firm level, leveraging extant research in the development of one hypothesis. We then examine the sources of financing and the relationship between the investor and investee, leading to five hypotheses. We conclude our country examination with population-level differences among all Italian adults, and then only those who are actively participating in the labor force.

NATIONAL CONTEXT: ITALY

Italy has a rich manufacturing heritage, a tradition of family-owned firms, and the lowest number of employees per firm in all of Europe (Mattiaci, Simoni, & Zanni, 2006). Italian SMEs outperform the large firm sector (Mediobanca-Unioncamere, 2005) and are present in most industrial districts (Fortis, 2004). The rate of female entrepreneurship in Italy is lower than the world and European averages (Reynolds et al., 2004). Females in Italy comprise 20% of entrepreneurs but 35.6% of the workforce (European Union, 2000). In 2002, the percentage of the working population of self-employed in Italy was 7.7% for women and 13.4% for men (Eurostat, 2002), and females' rates decreased between 1976 and 1996 (European Union, 2000). Females' salaries in Italy comprise 101% of males in the public sector, but only 89% in the private sector (Eurostat, 1999). The Italian government has promoted female entrepreneurship with the 1992 Law 215 entitled "Positive Action for Female Entrepreneurs." The law has three aims: (1) promote entrepreneurship and vocational training of female entrepreneurs, (2) support the creation and development of female entrepreneurship, and (3) promote the presence of female-run companies in diverse activity sectors. While there have been ethnographic studies of sex and entrepreneurship in Italy (e.g., Bruni, Gherardi, & Poggio, 2005), there is a need for further quantitative study to complement these perspectives.

ENTREPRENEURS: DEMOGRAPHICS
AND PERSONAL CONTEXT

A consistent finding in past research is that male and female entrepreneurs have different personalities, backgrounds, motivations, and sectors of activity (e.g., Brush, 1992; Kalleberg & Leicht, 1991; Watkins & Watkins, 1986). We now explore the entrepreneurs' demographics, personal context, firm type and financing sources.

Demographics

Women entrepreneurs are, on average, older than their male counterparts (Reynolds et al., 2004). Kovalainen (1995) found that females' tendency to start their businesses later in life was the result of family commitments. We contend that the interrupted nature of women's careers due to commitments to children, partners' careers, and taking care of elderly relatives draws females' attention away from career or entrepreneurial aspirations and toward commitments to family during the period between 18 and 34 years old. In Italy, women have lower educational qualifications than their male counterparts. In general, female entrepreneurs are less likely to possess relevant work experience (Watkins & Watkins, 1986). In Italy, women have a limited history of participating in the workforce. Casson (1982) argues that access to personal wealth is a key barrier to entrepreneurial activity and that a lack of personal wealth typically restricts the scale of entrepreneurial activity engaged in by the individual. Household income is a way of amassing wealth, which can be invested in the business. Women in Italy tend to make less than their male counterparts. Based on the above, we hypothesize:

H1a: *Female entrepreneurs will likely be older than male entrepreneurs.*

H1b: *Female entrepreneurs will be less likely to possess higher education degrees.*

H1c: *Female entrepreneurs will be less likely to work full or part time.*

H1d: *Female entrepreneurs will have lower household incomes.*

Personal Context

The ability to perceive opportunities in the environment is linked to the propensity to become an entrepreneur (Reynolds et al., 2004). Furthermore, vicarious experience occurs as individuals observe others whom they perceive to be similar who succeed through continued efforts (Bandura, 1986). Individuals who have entrepreneurs in their social networks are more likely to participate in entrepreneurial activity, as an entrepreneur (Arenius & Kovalainen, 2006; Reynolds et al., 2004) or as an informal investor (Szerb, Rappai, Makra, & Terjesen, in press). Thus, we expect:

H2a: *Female entrepreneurs will be less likely to perceive entrepreneurial opportunities, as compared to males.*

H2b: *Female entrepreneurs will likely have the skills and knowledge needed to start a new business, as compared to males.*

H2c: *Female entrepreneurs will likely have a "recent" entrepreneur in their personal network, as compared to males.*

H2d: *Female entrepreneurs will be more likely to report fear of failure as a reason not to start a business, as compared to males.*

Firm Type

A consistent finding in entrepreneurship studies is the propensity for female entrepreneurs to operate in service and retail sectors (Kalleberg & Leicht, 1991), which have traditionally high levels of female employment.

H3:   *Female entrepreneurs are more likely to start firms in service-related sectors.*

Finance

Most entrepreneurs start with relatively small absolute amounts of funds and rely on self-financing, access informal venture capital from family, friends, and "foolhardy" investors (Bygrave, 2005), and bootstrap their new ventures (Winborg & Landstrom, 2001).

Studies of sex discrimination in debt finance have produced mixed conclusions, with some evidence that supports the proposition that females are discriminated against in accessing finance (Carter & Rosa, 1998). A UK study found sex differences in business financing: Females were less likely to use overdrafts, bank loans, and supplier credit, while males use more capital at startup (Carter & Rosa, 1998). Furthermore, this study found that females were more likely to be refused bank credit based on a lack of business experience and domestic circumstances, whereas males were more likely to be refused credit based on their lack of education attainment and choice of business sector. Fabowale, Orser, and Riding (1995) found that females were more likely to perceive that they were being treated disrespectfully by lending officers, suggesting that females perceive sex discrimination. Based on the above literature, we expect differences between male and female entrepreneurs in terms of how they finance their new venture.

H4a: *In Italy, female entrepreneurs will expect to provide more of the required startup capital from their own financial resources, as compared to male entrepreneurs.*

H4b: *In Italy, female entrepreneurs will expect to raise their external finance from their immediate family, and not from other external sources of capital such as banks and governments programs, as compared to male entrepreneurs.*

Investee Relationship and Firm Type

A key area of interest in the research on informal investors is the relationship between the informal investor and the entrepreneur. Informal investors typically identify opportunities through personal and business networks. Knowing the entrepreneur personally is likely to make an investor feel more comfortable with sharing personal funds. Informal investment is hampered by poor familiarity with entrepreneurs (Mason & Harrison, 2002). External investors face a number of difficulties in identifying and investing in new ventures. These include information asymmetries between the entrepreneur and the investor, and expectation asymmetries between the entrepreneur and the investor (Mason & Harrison, 1999), and the liability of newness that characterizes new ventures (Aldrich & Fiol, 1994).

In a study of male and female business angels in the United Kingdom, Harrison and Mason (2005) concluded that female business angels differ from their male counterparts in only very limited respects and that sex is not a major issue in determining the supply of informal investment. Rather, Harrison and Mason (2005) report sex differences in networking behaviors, with females less well connected with or knowing other business angels. Female informal investors may prefer to finance entrepreneurs with whom they share strong personal ties as they may have less experience with informal investment, or less access to investment opportunities outside their personal social ties. Based on the above, we hypothesize:

H5a: *Female informal investors will be more likely to provide finance to members of their immediate family, and less likely to provide financing to work colleagues, as compared to male informal investors.*

H5b: *Female informal investors will be more likely to invest in service-related sectors.*

Population Level Differences

Reynolds et al. (2004) argued that personal context is an important determinant of propensity to engage in entrepreneurial activity. They demonstrated that individuals that perceive opportunity in their local environment, perceive that they have the knowledge and skills to start a business, and know a recent entrepreneur are significantly more likely to be entrepreneurs. That is, variation in entrepreneurial activity partly reflects variation in the personal context of the adult population in a country. Furthermore, females who know an entrepreneur are more likely to engage in entrepreneurial activity (Minniti et al., 2006).

H6a: *In Italy, females will be less likely to perceive entrepreneurial opportunities, as compared to males.*

H6b: *In Italy, females will be less likely to have the skills and knowledge needed to start a new business, as compared to males.*

H6c: *In Italy, females will be less likely to have a "recent" entrepreneur in their personal network, as compared to males.*

H6d: *In Italy, females will be more likely to report fear of failure as a reason not to start a business, as compared to males.*

As females in Italy have had less experience in the labor market, when compared to males, we are also interested in ascertaining if there are differences between employed females and employed males.

H7a: *In Italy, employed females will be less likely to perceive entrepreneurial opportunities, as compared to employed females.*

H7b: *In Italy, employed females will be less likely to have the skills and knowledge needed to start a new business, as compared to employed females.*

H7c: *In Italy, employed females will be less likely to have a "recent" entrepreneur in their personal network, as compared to employed females.*

H7d: *In Italy, employed females will be more likely to report fear of failure as a reason not to start a business, as compared to employed females.*

METHODOLOGY AND DATA

For this study, we use Global Entrepreneurship Monitor (GEM) telephone survey data of Italy's adult population in 1999, 2000, and 2001. The GEM study tracks entrepreneurship in over 40 countries, including Italy. In Italy, the 3 years of the survey resulted in a sample of 4,971 people, including 3,311 adults aged 18-64. We aggregate data from all 3 years (e.g., Acs, Szerb, Terjesen, & O'Gorman, 2007). (The survey data is publicly available at www.gemconsortium.org.) Previous reports from GEM Italy include Minniti (2000) and Minniti and Venturelli (2001).

Variables

Entrepreneurs are adults who self-identify as having, in the past year, undertaken some activities toward starting a new business, and who expect to own a share of the business, which has not paid any wages or salaries for more than 3 months. Basic demographic data includes *age* (based on year of birth); *education* (categorical variable based on highest level of education completed: no education, some secondary education, secondary degree, post-secondary education, and graduate degree); and *work status* (categorical variable based on current work status: full time or part time, part time only, retired or disabled, homemaker, student, or other). The GEM survey includes the following dichotomous (yes or no) personal context variables: *know an entrepreneur* ("You know someone personally who started a business in the past 2 years"); *good opportunities* ("In the next 6 months, there will be good opportunities for starting a business in the area where you live"); *skills* ("You have the knowledge, skill, and experience required to start a new business"); and *fear of failure* ("Fear of failure would prevent you from starting a business").

Entrepreneurs are asked to provide details of the financing, including, in euros, *personal investment provided* (scaled variable to the question, "How much of your own money, in total, do you expect to provide to this new business?"). *Financing sources* is based on the response to the following question: "Have you received or do you expect to receive money from any of the following to start this business: close family member, other relatives, work colleagues, an employer, friends or neighbors, banks or other financial institutions, government programs, or other?"

Firm type is separated into 10 categories: agriculture/forestry/hunting/fishing, mining/construction, manufacturing, transport/communications/utilities, wholesale/motor vehicle sales/repair, retail/hotel/management, finance/insurance/real estate, business services, health/education/social services, and consumer services.

Our analysis is based on *t*-tests and chi-squares, which were conducted using SPSS.

RESULTS

Demographics and Personal Context

In Italy, female entrepreneurs differ from male entrepreneurs in terms of education or work status (Table 4.1). We find no difference in terms of age; the mean age of Italian female entrepreneurs is just over 36 years, as compared to males who are, on average, almost 38 years of age. We reject H1a. We find that female entrepreneurs are more likely than the men to have graduate education, but less likely to have post-secondary education ($p < .10$). Thus, H1b is not fully supported. Female and male entrepreneurs also have significantly different current work status ($p < .001$). Females are

TABLE 4.1
Italian Entrepreneurs' Demographics

Variables	Entrepreneurs		Significance
	Female	Male	
Age of Entrepreneur (Mean)	36.33	37.97	None
	(n = 154)	(n = 215)	
Highest Education Completed	(n = 154)	(n = 215)	*
Some Secondary	33.0%	20.1%	
Secondary	31.6%	39.0%	
Post-Secondary	29.8%	37.0%	
Graduate	5.6%	3.9%	
Work Status	(n = 153)	(n = 214)	***
Full or Part-Time	45.1%	75.7%	
Retired or Disabled	3.3%	5.1%	
Homemaker	20.3%	0.5%	
Student	7.8%	4.2%	
Other	23.5%	14.5%	
Household Income	(n = 46)	(n = 41)	None
Highest Third	73.9%	53.7%	
Middle Third	17.4%	36.6%	
Lowest Third	52.9%	47.1%	
Firm Type	(n = 45)	(n = 48)	None
Agriculture/Forestry/Hunting/Fishing	13.3%	10.4%	
Mining/Construction	0.0%	8.3%	
Manufacturing	17.8%	14.6%	
Transport/Communications/Utilities	2.2%	10.4%	
Wholesale/Motor Vehicle Sales/Repair	2.2%	2.1%	
Retail/Hotel/Restaurant	24.4%	16.7%	
Finance/Insurance/Real Estate	2.2%	6.3%	
Business Services	20.0%	22.9%	
Health/Education/Social Services	11.1%	2.1%	
Consumer Services	6.7%	6.3%	
Personal Context			
Know an entrepreneur (% yes)	36.3%	63.0%	***
	(n = 124)	(n = 165)	
Good opportunities (% yes)	58.9%	60.7%	None
	(n = 129)	(n = 191)	
Skills (Have knowledge and skills to start)	55.7%	76.1%	**
(% yes)	(n = 70)	(n = 67)	
Fear of failure (% yes)	34.4%	29.3%	None
	(n = 122)	(n = 164)	

*** $p < .001$; ** $p < .01$; * $p < .05$; ‡ $p\_ .10$

less likely to be in full- or part-time employment, and are more likely to work as a homemaker, thus H1c is also true. There is no difference between male and female entrepreneurs' household incomes, thus H1d is rejected.

In terms of personal context, female entrepreneurs are significantly ($p < .001$) less likely to report knowing an individual who has started a business in the last 2 years: only 36% of female entrepreneurs report knowing another entrepreneur, compared to 63% for males. Females are significantly ($p < .01$) less likely to report that they have the knowledge and skills to start their own firms. We find no differences between female and male entrepreneurs in terms of perception of opportunity, and whether fear of failure would prevent them starting a business. Thus, H2a and H2c are supported, while H2b and H2d are rejected.

Firm Type and Finance Source

We do not find significant differences between the types of businesses started by males and females; however, female entrepreneurs are more likely to start firms in retail/hotel/restaurants, health/education/social services, and consumer services (Table 4.2). Male entrepreneurs are more likely to be starting businesses in mining/construction, transport/communications/utilities, and business services. We reject H3. We find no statistically significant differences between females and males in terms of where they expect to source their required capital, although females are more

TABLE 4.2
Demand: Italian Entrepreneurs' Financing Sources

Investment Variables	Entrepreneurs		Significance
	Female	Male	
Financing Sources			
Close Family (% yes)	42.1% (n = 19)	23.7% (n = 59)	None
Other Relatives, Kin (% yes)	5.0% (n = 20)	10.2% (n = 59)	None
Work Colleague (% yes)	5.0% (n = 20)	18.6% (n = 59)	None
Employer (% yes)	5.0% (n = 20)	5.2% (n = 58)	None
Friends/Neighbors (% yes)	5.0% (n = 20)	11.9% (n = 59)	None
Banks/Other Financial Institutions (% yes)	57.9% (n = 19)	50% (n = 58)	None
Government Programs (% yes)	15.8% (n = 19)	38.3% (n = 60)	None
Other (% yes)	15% (n = 20)	15.5% (n = 58)	None

$***p < .001; **p < .01; *p < .05; \ddagger p \_ .10$

likely to report wishing to turn to close family and banks, and less likely to turn to other relatives, work colleagues, government programs, and friends and neighbors. We reject H4a and H4b.

Population Level Differences

We find that the personal context of males and females in the population are different (Table 4.3). Italian females are less likely to know a recent entrepreneur ($p < .001$), perceive entrepreneurial opportunity ($p < .001$), report that they have the skills and knowledge needed to start a new business ($p < .001$), and that they fear failure ($p < .001$). This supports H5a, H5b, H5c, and H5d.

Finally, we find that employed females and employed males also differ in terms of entrepreneurial personal context (Table 4.4). Employed Italian females who are less likely to know an entrepreneur ($p < .001$) report that they have the skills and knowledge needed to start a new business ($p < .01$); and are more likely to fear failure ($p < .001$). Thus, H6a, H6c, and H6d are supported. There are no differences between males and females in the working population in terms of perceiving good opportunities, hence H6b is rejected.

TABLE 4.3
Personal Context of the Italian Adult Population

	Adults		
	Female	Male	Significance
Personal Context			
Know an entrepreneur (% yes)	27.0%	43.2%	***
	(n = 1331)	(n = 1298)	
Good opportunities (% yes)	44.4%	49.5%	*
	(n = 972)	(n = 1031)	
Skills (Have knowledge and skills to start)	26.7%	40.4%	***
(% yes)	(n = 786)	(n = 743)	
Fear of failure prevents startup (% yes)	42.5%	32.5%	***
	(n = 1240)	(n = 1235)	

*** $p < .001$; ** $p < .01$; * $p < .05$; ‡ $p_- .10$

TABLE 4.4
Personal Context of the Italian Adult Population Classified as Working (Either Full Time or Part Time)

	Adults		
	Female	Male	Significance
Personal Context			
Know an entrepreneur (% yes)	29.2%	70.8%	***
	(n = 499)	(n = 857)	
Good opportunities (% yes)	44.9%	48.7%	None
	(n = 370)	(n = 677)	
Skills (Have knowledge and skills to start)	32.3%	42.7%	**
(% yes)	(n = 263)	(n = 452)	
Fear of failure prevents startup (% yes)	40.1%	31.3%	***
	(n = 469)	(n = 820)	

***$p < .001$; **$p < .01$; *$p < .05$; ‡p _ .10

CONCLUSION

The results of this study highlight that there are differences between male and female entrepreneurs in Italy. Firms in Italy have generally been found to invest less in education than their northern European counterparts (European Commission, 2004). We find that females are more likely to start businesses in the service sectors of health, restaurants, and retail, which confirms to the general perception in the business community that females are more likely to pursue careers in service businesses. We find that there is no difference between age of male and female Italians. As not as many females as males know other entrepreneurs, this suggests that males utilize their personal networks to a higher extent.

REFERENCES

Acs, Z., Szerb, L., Terjesen, S., & O'Gorman, C. (2007). Could the Irish miracle be repeated in Hungary? *Small Business Economics.*

Aldrich, H. E., & Fiol, C. M. (1994). Fools rush in? The institutional context of industry creation. *Academy of Management Review, 19,* 645–670.

Bandura, A. (1986). *Social foundations of thought and action: A social cognitive theory.* Englewood Cliffs, NJ: Prentice Hall.

Bird, B., & Brush, C. (2002). A gendered perspective on organizational creation, *Entrepreneurship Theory and Practice, 26*(3), 41–65.

Bruni, A., Gherardi, S., & Poggio, P. (2005). *Gender and entrepreneurship: An ethnographic approach*. London: Routledge.

Brush, C. G. (1992). Research on women business owners: Past trends, a new perspective and future directions, *Entrepreneurship Theory and Practice, 16*(4), 5–30.

Bygrave, W. D., with Hunt, S. (2005). *Financing entrepreneurial ventures*. Global Entrepreneurship Monitor Financing report. Babson College and London Business School.

Carter, N. M., Brush, C. G., Greene, P. G., Gatewood, E., & Hart, M. M. (2003). Women entrepreneurs who break through to equity financing: The influence of human, social and financial capital. *Venture Capital, 5*(1), 1–28.

Carter, N. M., & Williams, M. L. (2005). Comparing social feminism and liberal feminism: The case of new firm growth. In J. E. Butler (Ed.), *New perspectives on women entrepreneurs*. Greenwich, CT: Information Age.

Carter, S., & Rosa, P. (1998). The financing of male and female owned-businesses, *Entrepreneurship and Regional Development, 10*(3), 225–241.

Casson, M. (1982). *The entrepreneur: An economic theory*. Oxford, UK: Martin Robertson.

Center for Women's Business Research. (2005). *Top facts about women owned businesses*. Silver Spring, MD: Author.

European Union (EU). (2000). *Entrepreneurship interculturalisation project: Networking for global opportunities and development in Austria, India and Italy*.

European Commission (EC). (2004). *Action plan: The European agenda for entrepreneurship*. COM 11.02.04. Brussels: Author.

Eurostat. (1999). *Salary differences (M/F) in the EU*.

Eurostat. (2002). *EU labour force survey: Self-employment in the EU*.

Fabowale, L., Orser, B., & Riding, A. (1995). Gender, structural factors, and credit Terms between Canadian small businesses and financial institutions. *Entrepreneurship Theory and Practice, 19*(4), 41–65.

Fortis, M. (2004). *Pilastri, colonne, distretti: una tassonomia delle principali imprese italiane*. Economia e politica industriale, *n. 121*.

Greene, P. G., Hart, M. H., Gatewood, E. J., Brush, C. G., & Carter, N. M. (2004). *Women entrepreneurs: moving front and center: An overview of research and theory*. Working Paper.

Harrison, R.T., & Mason, C M. (2005, April). *Does gender matter?: Women business angels and the supply of entrepreneurial finance*. Working Paper, Centre for Entrepreneurship Research, University of Edinburgh Management School/Hunter Centre for Entrepreneurship, University of Strathclyde.

Kalleberg, A. L., & Leicht, K. T. (1991). Gender and organizational performance: Determinants of small business survival and success. *Academy of Management Journal, 34*, 136–161.

Kovalainen, A. (1995). *At the margins of the economy: Women's self-employment in Finland, 1960–1990*. Avebury, UK: Aldershot.

Mason, C. M., & Harrison, R. T. (1999). An overview of informal venture capital research. *Venture Capital, 1*(2), 95–100.

Mason C. M., & Harrison, R. T. (2002). Barriers to investment in the informal venture capital sector, *Entrepreneurship and Regional Development, 14*(3), 271–287.

Mattiacci, A., Simoni, C., & Zanni, L. (2006). Italian SME international strategies: State of the art and some empirical evidence. In L.-P. Dana, M. Han, V. Ratten,

& I. Welpe (Eds.), *A theory of internationalisation for European entrepreneurship.* Cheltenham, UK: Edward Elgar.

Mediobanca-Unioncamere. (2005). *Le medie imprese industriali italiane (1996–2002), Novembre.* Milano: Ufficio Studi Mediobanca e Ufficio Studi Unioncamere.

Minniti, M. (2000) *National entrepreneurship assessment: Italy.* 1999 Executive Report. Babson College.

Minniti, M., Arenius, P., & Langowitz, N. (2006). *Global Entrepreneurship Monitor 2005 Report on Women and Entrepreneurship.*

Minniti, M., & Venturelli, P. (2001). *National entrepreneurship assessment: Italy.* 2000 Executive Report.

OECD (Organization for Economic Cooperation and Development). (2000). *OECD Small and Medium Enterprise Outlook.* Paris: Author.

OECD. (2001). *Female entrepreneurship indicator: Benchmarking enterprise policy: Results from the 2001 scoreboard.* Commission Staff Working Document, Brussels.

Reynolds, P. D., Bygrave, W. D., & Autio, E. (2004). *Global Entrepreneurship Monitor: 2003 Executive Report.* Babson College and London Business School.

Szerb, L., Rappai, G., Makra, Z., & Terjesen, S. (in press). Informal investments in transition: Motivations, characteristics, and classifications in Eastern Europe. *Small Business Economics.*

Watkins, J. M., & Watkins, D. S. (1986). The female entrepreneur: her background and determinants of business choice—some British data. In S. Curran, J. Stanworth, & D. Watkins (Eds.), *The survival of the small firm, Vol. 1: The economics of survival and entrepreneurship* (pp. 220–232). Aldershot, UK: Gower.

Winborg, J., & Landstrom, H. (2001). Financial bootstrapping in small businesses: Examining small business managers' resource acquisition behaviors. *Journal of Business Venturing, 16*(3), 235–254.

CHAPTER 5

WOMEN ENTREPRENEURS IN MOROCCO

Vanguards of Change in the Muslim World

Kenneth R. Gray and Doris H. Gray

INTRODUCTION

Women are changing the face of modern business. They are at the forefront of the service sector, the fastest growing sector of the economy. Women entrepreneurs have created organizations that serve their constituents and their employees. They have instituted innovative systems and schedules. Yet the business world is still a male domain, particularly so in the Muslim world. This research investigates women and entrepreneurship in Morocco.

As argued by the United Nations Development Report on Arab Human Development (2003), "the potential for developing the knowledge capabilities of Arab countries is enormous—not only because of their untapped human capital, but also because of their rich cultural, linguistic and intellectual heritage." We begin with introducing entrepreneurship as a new frontier for women in Morocco. This section is followed by an examination of data from our study of women entrepreneurs in this North African

The Perspective of Women's Entrepreneurship in the Age of Globalization, pages 55–67
Copyright © 2007 by Information Age Publishing

country, elaborating on responses from interviews concerning their reasons for becoming entrepreneurs, their successful practices, and finally, the business strategies they pursue.

Western business managers cannot hope to function successfully in Muslim countries, in the long run, with scant understanding of Islamic cultures (Abbasi & Hollman, 1993). Understanding cultural norms and everyday routines is important for building relationships in the international business arena.

WOMEN IN MOROCCAN CULTURE

Women in Morocco can best be described as a minority as explained by Leila Ahmed who has applied the western concept of minority to women in the Muslim world. She writes: "In establishment Islamic thought, women, like minorities, are defined as different from and, in their legal rights, lesser than Muslim men. Unlike non-Muslim men, who might join the master-class by converting, women's differentness and inferiority within the system are immutable" (Ahmed, 1993, p. 7). Women's position in society follows from women as a group dominated by men. This inferiority is often inscribed in the legal code that governs activities and practices in the nation. As a result, women are expected to be docile without much capacity to contribute to commercial society. This unequal status is written into law in most Muslim countries, particularly in the Personal Status Code. As women are historically considered of a lower status in Moroccan society, men assert their power over them. Up until recent times, women have been viewed as a dominated minority who lack a voice in the society. This is mainly derived from the deeply rooted foundation of the patriarchal society. Gender equality is at the forefront of political, social, and economic change in Morocco. The 2004 major reform of the Personal Status Code law, or family law in Western parlance, legally altered the conception and role of women in Moroccan society. In essence, the understanding of family was changed from a unit presided over by a man to being a unit between two legal equals. Reforming the law is certainly only one step in a long process that requires implementation of the new laws and changing the mindset of people in Morocco. As the family law pertains to women's rights on various levels, it has far-reaching consequences for women's public role. Changes to the Personal Status Code, called *moudawana* in Morocco, pertained to the raising of the marriage age for girls to 18 years, restricting the practice of polygamy, allowing women to initiate a divorce, women's rights with regard to inheritance, and abolition of the concept of "wali" or guardian. Previously, a woman was considered under the lifelong tutelage of a man, first her father, then her husband, brother, or another elder male in the family. The wali had consent to such mundane matters as obtaining a passport or opening a business. Thus, the change of the family law also affects the area of women entrepreneurship. Indeed, the status of women is at the heart of the process of democratic change in Morocco. Unlike in other Middle Eastern and North African countries, women's organizations in Morocco are free to advocate for any cause. Thus, Morocco can be viewed as an engine of change in the Middle-East and North African (MENA) region.

As in most Islamic countries that have been colonies, or in the case of Morocco, a protectorate of a Western country—mostly France and Great Britain—a dual legal system was established. The civil, criminal, and commercial legal systems are largely modeled after French and Spanish law. The Personal Status Code, or family law, remained a separate entity, based on religious law, or *shariah*. The 2004 change of the Personal Status Code in Morocco gave this country one of the most liberal family laws in the MENA region. What makes the Personal Status Code (PSC) reform in Morocco all the more remarkable is the fact that the legal reform signifies a reinterpretation of the religion of Islam. This is because the monarch holds the dual role of Head of State and "Commander of the Faithful." This means that the king is also the highest religious authority in the country. When announcing the reform, King Mohamed VI emphasized that the reform was based on a new understanding of the sacred scriptures.

This chapter hopes to expose simplified conceptions of the Arab world by exploring entrepreneurship as an emerging trend for Muslim women. It is central to recognize that Muslim social customs are based on the societal and familial dominance of males. Furthermore, Islamic mores prohibit most mingling of the sexes in public. As a result, women are usually not part of business transactions for traditional Muslims. Ironically, this cultural foundation (strong male role-models and blocked entry to business ventures) may give rise to women entertaining entrepreneurial pursuits and establishing businesses independent of males. In fact, Brenner (1987, p. 95) notes that "entrepreneurship inevitably implies a deviation from customary behavior" that individuals engage in because they see themselves as disadvantaged from others in their society and want to catch up through business innovation.

A NEW FRONTIER FOR MOROCCAN WOMEN

Entrepreneurship research argues that different cultures carry different beliefs about the desirability and feasibility of beginning a new enterprise (cf. McGrath, MacMillan, & Scheinberg, 1992). It is imperative to recognize that people from cultures, other than one's own, may have differing values and belief systems. Moreover, Westerners should be cognizant that Muslims, like Christians, Jews, or adherents to any religious or cultural group for that matter, are not a monolithic group. There are significant intragroup differences within Islamic societies. Without this understanding, the view of Muslim customs may become distorted. In Morocco, the rise of political Islam is a significant force that is countered by government efforts to "modernize" society more in line with Western values. Again, the question of the role of women is central to the political discourse.

In the recent past, Morocco set a historical precedent when its elected Parliament convened with 33 women members, the largest number ever (United Nations Development Program, 2003). This precedent was the result of affirmative action for women—designating a set number of allocations for women on national lists. The *Atlas of Women in the World* (Seager, 2003) offers a revealing international social analysis of women. For instance, compared to Saudi Arabia and Iran who rank under 30%, Morocco has the highest percentage of all women who work for pay (40–49%). Unfortunately, Morocco also has the highest rate of adult women who are illiterate (51–75%) when contrasted to Saudi Arabia and Iran (26–50%). Ironically, 40–59% of all university students in Morocco are women. Taken together, these data present an enigma: highest percentage of women who work for pay, highest percentage of illiterate women, second highest percentage of female university students, and women's empowerment at the executive levels of government. This makes Morocco an intriguing setting to investigate entrepreneurial pursuits of Muslim women in business.

ENVIRONMENTAL CONTEXT: PUBLIC AND PRIVATE

An additional cultural value that impacts women entrepreneurs in Morocco, as in other Muslim countries, is that the public is explicitly public, and the private is equally explicitly private. They are two separate worlds in which the rules of engagement are different. The public refers to the street, men's space, everything is up for grabs, and every man for himself. This is contrasted with the private, which refers to the home, wherein all relationships are accounted for.

Arabs and North Africans are renowned for their hospitality; however, life in the streets is often rude and unruly. The street (public) belongs to no one and to everyone. Out in the public sphere, women are particularly vulnerable. They are encroaching on men's space and they need to appear as unobtrusive as possible. In recent years, the veil has made a comeback in Morocco, particularly among young, educated women. Among other things, being veiled affords women a measure of respect and safety in the public domain.

The essence of street life is profane. Without the matrix of family relationships, or those between guest and host that prevail in the home, there is virtually no protocol for the street. Shopkeepers and other people who work with the public do not expect friendliness, nor do they often manifest it. Excessive friendliness or familiarity in public with strangers may be viewed as weakness or foolishness.

Private life, by contrast, is different. A Moroccan's home is her fortified inner sanctum. The very architecture reveals the sharp separation between street (public) and home (private): windows are few, and always shuttered if they are at street level. In neighborhoods that have space, high walls surround the house to keep out inquiring eyes. The exteriors of houses are often nondescript, suggesting nothing of the spaciousness or sumptuousness that may lie within.

MODERN MOROCCAN SOCIETY

Today, women are participating in all occupational fields in Morocco. They can be seen climbing the social ladder as they have more opportunities in job situations. For example, women now no longer encounter as many barriers to education; they have access to higher levels of education and more women are occupying important positions in organizations. The Qur'an, the sacred scripture of Islam, has been interpreted to recommend that men and women have equal opportunities for education and political participation rights as well as duties.

With the ushering in of change through globalization, sometimes when Moroccan women meet male friends in the streets, clubs, and cafés (many belonging to the same social class as their male friends—rich, "modern," and educated), they greet each other with kisses on the cheek, much like in the French style. The values that underlie this are modernism, women's liberty, and the behavioral relationships among women/girls and men/boys of the same (usually upper) social class. In fact, Morocco's cultural values, as values of a Muslim- and Arab-influenced country, are being transformed and in many instances replaced by Western values—in an era of globalization and standardization of cultural values and norms. Moreover, since the colonial era, people (especially those in the higher social classes) of former colonies such as Morocco have been trying to overcome their feeling of inferiority by emulating Western modes (Fernea, 1998).

Thus, women who choose to follow an independent path, in spite of religious, socioeconomic, and legal obstacles, are those who stand on their own achievements and successes in society. These women have several entrepreneurial traits that can be identified: a high need for achievement, autonomy, independence, moderate risk propensity, and experience of rejection from society. In the following section, our analysis of Moroccan entrepreneurs will reflect these entrepreneurial propensities.

A LOOK AT WOMEN ENTREPRENEURS IN MOROCCO

Women in Morocco constitute about 50% of the overall population, and make up more than a quarter of the labor force (GEM, 2005). In recent times, labor force participation of women has increased in both urban and rural areas, and is strong in the agricultural sector including fishing and forestry. Women with higher qualifications are employed in the service sectors. However, the female unemployment rate has increased over the past 5 years to 27.6% (World Bank, Morocco Gender Update, 2002).

The creation of enterprises run by women is a phenomenon that dates back to the 1980s and 1990s in Morocco. In several studies, experts estimated the number of female Moroccan entrepreneurs who own or run a company in various sectors to add up to 5,000 and to represent about 0.5% of total female employment in formal economic and about 10% of all enterprises (GEM, 2005). These figures do not take into account the micro enterprise sector where women's entrepreneurship activities are also increasing and are supported by national and international development programs.

In our studies, several categories of responses to queries of women entrepreneurs were found and are presented in the following three sections: impetus, independence, and strategies (Gray, 2001; Gray & Finley-Hervey, 2005). Impetus refers to women's motivation for entering into entrepreneurship. Some were "pulled" and others "pushed." Independence refers the ability of women to act autonomously from their husbands and family. This ability is greatly circumscribed by the public and private dichotomy in Islamic societies. Finally, strategies look at successful business practices.

IMPETUS FOR ENTREPRENEURSHIP

What propels women toward self-employment? We found two influences of entrepreneurial intent: positive pull and negative push (Timmons, 1999; Vesper, 1990). Positive pull factors that draw individuals into self-employment are largely opportunity driven. This may come from a potential partner, mentor, parent, investor, or customer particularly, a market opportunity. Thus, one ventures to pursue an idea for new products through a new business startup. Negative push influences refer to the negative aspects of a potential entrepreneur's present economic/employment situation that cause him or her to look for something else, either another job or a startup. Here, one is forced to pursue entrepreneurial activity and may not have other choices. Several empirical studies characterize entrepreneurs as misfits, rejects from society, or displaced individuals (Gilad & Levine, 1986; Gray, Cooley, Lutabingwa, Mutai-Kaimenyi, & Oyugi, 1996; Shapero, 1975). Amit (1994) proposed that pull entrepreneurs may perform better than push entrepreneurs, and those that can be classified as both push and pull may be the most motivated of all.

Research shows an association between parent's occupation (i.e., a strong self-employed parent figure) and offspring entrepreneurship (cf. Hisrich & Peers, 1991). This may be a strong pull determinant of Moroccan women choosing to become entrepreneurs since Muslim cultures are patrilineal. Gray (2001) notes that "frustration with the government or private work environments is very likely to push women to take steps to launch their own business," which results in an increasing percentage of Moroccan women entrepreneurs.

Two-thirds of women entrepreneurs in Morocco were pulled and one-third was pushed into entrepreneurship due to various circumstances (Gray & Finley-Hervey, 2005). Women were pulled or drawn into self-employment due to an "opportunity to buy a business" or they spotted a "good market opportunity." With some, they inherited a family business or their business involved their field of educational study like pharmacy or dentistry. The pulled entrepreneur is opportunity driven. This means that they see a market opportunity and pursue it.

Others were pushed into entrepreneurship or gained the entrepreneurial driving force because they had "lost their jobs" or saw "no opportunity for advancement" in some cases. Others said that "their husband died" and they had no alternative, as they "needed money." This is exceptional considering the phenomenal sociopolitical and economic barriers they had to overcome. As a comparison, in an ongoing companion study, male entrepreneurs were found to be "pushed" into entrepreneurship at a rate of only 10%, while 33.3% of women sampled were found to be "pushed" into entrepreneurship.

Almost half the women (46.6%) identified the market opportunity by their chosen vocation or skill. A smaller percentage considered a void in the market or lack of competition (26.6%) as an opening into entrepreneurship.

INDEPENDENCE—PUBLIC VERSUS PRIVATE

We see that the women use their parents' or husbands' ability to travel abroad to further their own economic activities. It is interesting that women use their dependence on their parents or husbands to be able to travel abroad to provide the basis for their future "independence" should their husbands die or they become divorced.

The social networks of these women entrepreneurs are also important. Without the social networks, entrepreneurial women would have no customers because women are frowned upon if seen selling publicly. Lower economic status women may use their social networks to sell goods, but they can also sell as street and market vendors. This gives lower economic status women access to a much larger customer base that may include persons from all economic strata, whereas middle- and upper-middle-class women must generate their customers from only within their own economic class.

Women operate in "public" and "private" environmental contexts. One of the observations about women who engage in commerce is in regard to economic contribution to the household. The more they contribute, they more autonomy they create for themselves. Women can assert their right to operate in public spheres when they make significant contributions to the household economy and when they are able to maintain control not only of their productive labor, but also of the marketing of whatever they produce. The result is that due to the importance of their economic activities, women can also decide how to spend the money they earn; can travel to visit relatives by themselves; or decide to seek health care for themselves and their children. In other words, women's independent economic activity gives them power in other aspects of their lives.

The situation for middle- and upper-middle-class Moroccan women appears to be different in several regards. In understanding these differences, we extend our knowledge of the connection between economic autonomy and personal autonomy as well as expand our knowledge of the concepts of public and private. There appear to be at least two contradictions: (1) Upper-middle class Moroccan women seem to use their dependence on their spouse (for travel and access to goods to sell) in order to create a sort of bank account of independence for future needs. Since the income they generate is not needed for the current support of their families and households, generating income does not necessarily generate personal autonomy. Furthermore, (2) the entrepreneurial activities in which they engage would bring them sanctions from both their husbands and other women of their social class should they attempt to sell in a public context (market, street vending), but are supported as long as the selling is private (amongst themselves). Women of lower economic classes who engage in marketing are said to cross the boundaries of private and public as their culture defines them. But women of higher economic status are still constrained by the boundaries of their culturally defined public and private domains.

It was found that there are two steps to entrepreneurial success: (1) obtain proficiency (i.e., spirituality, education, and strategy); and (2) utilization of those skill-sets (i.e., experience) to start up one's own business enterprise. Essentially, the route to successful entrepreneurship rests on four principles: spirituality, education, strategy, and experience.

Key lessons learned by Moroccan women entrepreneurs were that obtaining proficiency and utilizing skill-sets greatly supported their entrepreneurial pursuits. Spirituality taps the extent to which religious beliefs or customs prime and sustain an individual in self-employment. It refers to the virtues of faith, persevering, and sacrificing. Education involves the level of academic preparation a woman attains prior to becoming an entrepreneur. It includes developing the competencies and business skills for self-employment. Strategy is both plan (i.e., spotting needs including assessing growth and financial need, preparing carefully) and ploy (e.g., being tactical and knowing when to cash in and when to hold on). It includes maintaining patience, scrutinizing situations, and properly appropriating trust in people. In this case, experience centers on enterprise operational issues. It examines the utilization of all the previous factors: spirituality, education, and strategy. Experience encompasses the degree to which operations are constrained or liberated by religion; operations are improved by educational skills; operational longevity is increased or decreased by a chosen strategy. In sum, experience implies executing your plan. Following the four pillars of spirituality, education, strategy, and experience may pave the path to entrepreneurial success for women in Morocco (see Figure 5.1).

STRATEGIES USED BY MOROCCAN WOMEN ENTREPRENEURS

The decision to expand a business or close a business depends on many factors, some of them beyond the control of the business owner. First, we should look at the macro-economic conditions under which the firm operates. The Moroccan macro-economic environment has been very harsh in the past 10 years, with a great deal of government control of businesses. GNP per capita in the country was greatly affected by drought and poor economic performance, the tragedy of September 11, and the terrorist attack in Casablanca in May 2003. This has led to a sharp decline in tourism to this country. Also, business strategy is affected by the business lifecycle and for entrepreneurs, the family lifecycle. Many businesses are begun with the main purpose of providing for one's family. Once this objective is secured, there is little reason to pursue growth strategies. From our interviews, Moroccan women entrepreneurs employed numerous strategies to

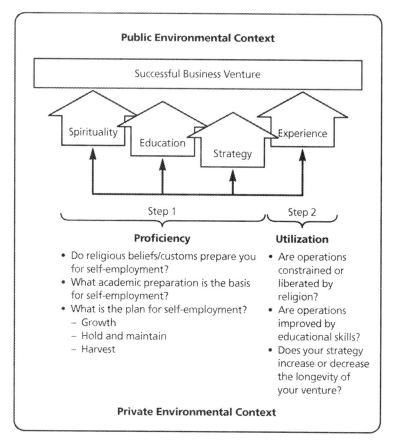

Figure 5.1.   A model of women entrepreneurship in Morocco.

avoid problems and ensure the longevity of their businesses. An analysis of responses from Moroccan women entrepreneurs shows a pattern of three basic strategies: growth, hold-and-maintain, or harvest. The growth strategy involves expanding an enterprise's relative competitive position. Expansion can be accomplished by investing in resources to develop new competencies and can be very expensive. A hold-and-maintain strategy involves protecting one's investment from aggressive competition and looking for any opportunity or weakness to take the lead among competitors. Lastly, the harvest strategy entails reducing assets to a minimum, forgoing investment, and extracting as much as possible for immediate profits.

Our research found that there is a strong desire to expand operations. The vast majority (87%) of Moroccan women entrepreneurs indicated that they would either expand or maintain their operations. Over half (53.3%) of the entrepreneurs expressed an inclination to expand. One third

(33.3%) desired to hold-and-maintain, while the remaining minority (13.3%) noted a preference to harvest or cash in their investment.

Women in Morocco account for more than 13 million of a total population of 30 million. Those who are lawyers, medical doctors, politicians, artists, entrepreneurs, and so on, represent the Morocco of today, and prepare for the Morocco of tomorrow. There are social and economic middle- and upper-middle-class Moroccan women who engage in informal economic activities (more like the Morocco of yesterday). These are the "push entrepreneurs," who follow this path to ensure their future survival and well-being of themselves and their children should their husbands die, take a second wife, or divorce them. Even though Moroccan men who take other wives or divorce a wife are in theory required to provide support for their children, without independent wealth, women may be at the mercy of a less than forthcoming man. Because of their husbands' status, the social pressure is such that it is not possible for these women to take employment outside of the home in order to create their own wealth. But they can generate independent wealth through entrepreneurial activities. The income generated through economic activities provides these Moroccan women insurance for their continuing well-being should they be divorced or become one of two or more wives.

CONCLUSION: VANGUARD OF CHANGE IN THE MUSLIM WORLD

Legal changes in Morocco concerning women and the family law have great impact on entrepreneurial opportunities. This chapter has explored Moroccan women operating businesses within the context of their culture based on Islam. As global business trade and relations continue to increase, it is essential that Westerners examine their perceptions and eliminate as much bias as possible. Often we find that views of Muslim customs may be distorted by presentations in the mass media. Our research is one step toward educating interested individuals about the changing role of Muslim women.

Additional research is warranted to explore the full utilization of women in the workforce, especially since women comprise 50% of the Moroccan population and 41% of them are economically active (Seager, 2003). This study reveals the importance of studying entrepreneurial activity and culture together; however, follow-up studies should explore additional sources of entrepreneurial influence and examine a wider variety of cultures. Women entrepreneurs are a growing international trend and women in Morocco are not an exception.

One key practical implication of our studies is the potential to cultivate cooperative relationships between universities within predominantly Islamic countries and U.S. universities. Given the opportunity for international cooperation, small business and entrepreneurship training adapted to sociocultural differences may offer a great value to women pursuing entrepreneurial ventures in Morocco. One approach may be the development of academic programs and partnership between Moroccan institutions of higher learning with those outside of that country. This approach will also create a reciprocal international learning experience, which results in an enhanced understanding of entrepreneurial activities across social cultures. The women themselves should participate in actions that are to be undertaken to enhance their capacity. The goal is empowerment of a significant portion of the populations in regards to national development. The empowerment of female entrepreneurs through increased self-sufficiency should be a central goal of intervention programs.

REFERENCES

Abbasi, S. M., & Hollman, K. W. (1993). Business success in the Middle East. *Management Decision, 31*(1), 55–60.

Ahmed, L. (1993). Women and gender in Islam: Historical roots of a modern debate. New Haven, CT: Yale University Press.

Amit, R. (1994). "Push" and "pull" entrepreneurs. *Frontiers of Entrepreneurship Research.* Available from www.babson.edu/entrep/fer/papers94/amit.htm

Brenner, R. (1987). National policy and entrepreneurship: The statesman's dilemma. *Journal of Business Venturing, 2*(2), 95–101.

Fernea, E. W. (1998). *In search of Islamic feminism.* New York: Anchor Books.

Gender and Entrepreneurship Markets (GEM). (2005). *GEM Country Brief— Morocco 2005.* Cairo: International Finance Corporation.

Gilad, B., & Levine, P. (1986). A behavioral model of entrepreneurial supply. *Journal of Small Business Management, 24*(4), 44–53.

Gray, K., & Finley-Hervey, J. (2005). Women entrepreneurs in Morocco: Debunking stereotypes and discerning strategies. *International Entrepreneurship and Management Journal,* No. 1, 203–217.

Gray, K. R. (2001). Women entrepreneurs in Morocco: A preliminary investigation. *North African Studies, 6*(4), 64–74.

Gray, K. R., Cooley, W., Lutabingwa, J., Mutai-Kaimenyi, B., & Oyugi, L. A. (1996). *Entrepreneurship in micro-enterprises.* Lanham, MD: University Press of America.

Hisrich, R., & Peers, M. (1991). *Entrepreneurship.* Homewood, IL: Irwin.

McGrath, R., MacMillan, I., & Scheinberg, S. (1992). Elitists, risk-takers, and rugged individualists? An exploratory analysis of cultural differences between entrepreneurs and non-entrepreneurs. *Journal of Business Venturing, 7,* 115–135.

Seager, J. (2003). *The Penguin atlas of women in the world.* Hong Kong: Penguin Books.

Shapero, A. (1975). The displaced, uncomfortable entrepreneur. *Psychology Today*, *9*(6), 83–88.

Timmons, J. (1999). *New venture strategies: Entrepreneurship for the 21st century* (5th ed.). Burr Ridge, IL: Irwin-McGraw-Hill.

United Nations Development Program. (2003). *Arab human development report 2003: Building a knowledge society*. Amman, Jordan: National Press.

Vesper, K. H. (1990). *New venture strategies*. Upper Saddle River, NJ: Prentice Hall.

CHAPTER 6

WOMEN ENTREPRENEURS AND DEVELOPMENT IN NIGERIA

Priscilla M. Achakpa

INTRODUCTION

To work for yourself, to be your own boss, and to run your own business has become the choice of many Nigerians since the failure of the Structural Adjustment Program in 1986. The current trend in the public sector of "downsizing" and "right-sizing" of formal wage-paying jobs has forced both men and women to opt for self-employment.

"Entrepreneur" is a term used broadly in connection with innovative and creative modern industrial business leaders. It is used to refer to a man or woman who sees business opportunities and takes advantage of the scarce resources to use them profitably. It is she or he alone who bears the noninsurable risks in the enterprise, and it is she or he who provides the human and material resources in the business objective.

Worldwide, there are people working in conditions that should not exist in this 21st century, for income that is barely enough for survival. For instance, 550 million people can not work their way out of extreme poverty (UN, 2005). Home-based workers and rural women spend back-breaking

The Perspective of Women's Entrepreneurship in the Age of Globalization, pages 69–76
Copyright © 2007 by Information Age Publishing
All rights of reproduction in any form reserved.

hours working on family farm land, often for no payment at all. The women, who constitute over 60% of the working class, engage in the informal sector, which is characterized by poor pay and job insecurity. Yet it is their work that holds families and communities together

While globalization has brought new opportunities to those with skills required in the high-tech global economy, it has deepened insecurity and poverty for many others, especially African women, who are constrained by family, community, and cultural values. It is a sobering fact to consider that as economies grow, formal work is increasingly becoming informal and workers lose job security as well as medical and other benefits. This has reduced the likelihood of obtaining formal employment with "footloose" companies, shifting production to unregulated zones, employing workers in informal contracts or with no benefits.

With some exceptions, literature has tended to underestimate the importance of women's work, especially in developing countries. At the same time, HIV/AIDS has in many countries pulled women out of production to take care of the ill and the dying (Heyzer et al., 2004; UNAIDS, 2004). Despite the sociocultural, political, and economic factors responsible for obstructing women's involvement in paid work, there is no doubt that more women are entering the labor force. This is as a result of the International Women's Movement, especially after the UN women's conference in Nairobi in 1985 and Beijing in 1995. Consequently, as nations were becoming parties to international conventions on human rights and gender equity, women resorted to public sectors as the only hope for formal employment. However, today, many countries have adopted privatization as a means of achieving economic growth, which implies the loss of employment, or joining the private sector.

To be an entrepreneur, therefore, one has to possess some psychological traits, which are either latent and could be aroused through training or through which training could be built upon.

WOMEN IN DEVELOPMENT

Records show that women comprise over half the world's population. They make a major contribution to the *development* of the world through their industrious nature. Hence the level of development of any country can be said to rely largely on the productivity of women through their active involvements in business and management.

WOMEN IN AGRICULTURE

In poorer countries of the developing world, women are largely involved in subsistence agriculture and earn supplemental income for the family through the sale of surplus food in the local markets. Eighty percent of Africa's food for the family and the market is grown by 100 million rural women, implying that each woman produces more than 3 metric tons of food per annum. Through the use of better farming methods and better seed varieties, increases in agricultural produce have been registered, hence more surpluses for the market. This has further boosted the development of agro-based industries such as processing and manufacturing. This does not only reduce post-harvest losses but also increases the shelf life of agricultural products and improves food security.

WOMEN AS CAREGIVERS

Societies have positioned women as mothers and caregivers, which they have, today, turned into opportunity to educate their children and equip them with the skills required in the labor market. Some women have sought employment as domestic workers and child day-care agents in order to sustain their families and make further investments. This also accords more women the opportunity to actively engage in business and other forms of development ventures besides their family roles.

As a housewife and mother, she has the sole responsibility of caring for the family, especially in war-torn countries. She has to get water for domestic chores, general clean-up of the surroundings, provision of first-aid needs of the family, and gathering of firewood, among others, which have no doubt supported the family. In addition, she gives her husband all the attention he deserves.

WOMEN AS ENTREPRENEURS

In the business sector, women are involved in different types of business activities ranging from operating business centers, firms, saloons, restaurants, tailoring centers, and sales of food, textiles, and other goods in local markets toward economic self-sufficiency. Most of these businesses provide employment opportunities and at times operate as centers of apprenticeship cum internship. In most countries in the developing world, it contributes to approximately 30–50% of the national gross domestic product (GDP).

A critical survey of the markets and streets of the urban areas will attest to the high level of women involvement in the economic development of Nigeria. This has also led to women forming different associations under which they carry out their businesses and through which the government can easily reach them in stirring them toward economic self-reliance and self-sufficiency. For instance, the women of Benue State have formed a group called the Branda Associations, which simply means the buying and selling of grains in major markets across the country. These associations, like the others, at market places regulate the level of product distribution and prices across the state. It is true that when the business sector of our economy is fully dominated by women, it will be well organized and it will be the fueling factor of our society—an engine for national development. This has been the focus of the Women Environmental Program: to motivate women to form associations/cooperatives for better understanding of their undertakings, high productivity, and improvement of their standard of living.

WOMEN'S ACTION THROUGH ASSOCIATIONS

In this era of gender equity and women empowerment, more women have come together and have embarked on the formation of Content Standards and Objectives policies (CSO). At the national level, women have formed a myriad of organizations, including professional associations of women doctors, engineers, scientists, and entrepreneurs. Some of these organizations are Action For Development (ACFODE), Forum for African Women Educationalists–Uganda (FAWEU), Uganda Women's Network (UWONET), and Federation of Women Lawyers (FIDA). These have, besides providing employment, greatly empowered communities through financial assistance, skill acquisition, legal aid, and capacity building. They have also contributed to the improvement of working conditions, which is a motivating factor and results in increased and improved production. At the local level, there are numerous clubs engaging in savings, farming, income-generating projects, handicrafts, and other functions, depending on the needs and priorities of members.

More still, CSOs such as Women in Peacebuilding Network (WIPNET), West Africa Network for Peacebuilding (WANEP), Center for Peace building and Socio-Economic Resources Development (CePSERD), Justice Development and Peace Commission (JDPC), World Education Program (WEP), Commonwealth Accounting Policies and Procedures (CAPP), The Center for Conflict Resolution (CECORE), and Agency for Cooperation and Research in Development (ACORD) have embarked on peace-building networks, especially on intra-national conflicts, as a remedy for the poor performance of the private sector. For a long time, women have suffered more as victims of war, yet many families derive their livelihood from their activities. Are men less victims of war? In what specific ways has war affected women in Nigeria? And because of historical division of labor, women have a more hands-on approach to problem solving and have been actively involved in the process of conflict resolution and negotiations on peace building. Development in the developing world has been largely hindered by insecurity and political instability. There is, however, no doubt that peace building creates a favorable environment for investment and economic development.

WOMEN IN ENVIRONMENT

The environmental pillar of Agenda 21 on sustainable development focuses on renewing vigor on observing the environmental rights of the poor. Women, as the major component of the poor, are also the major associates of the environment. Achieving sustainable development requires addressing inequality between women and men in the distribution of resources. Given that most developing countries have agro-based economies, land is the major productive asset for subsistence, export and raw material production. The contribution of CEDAW in improving women's accessibility to land has largely contributed to improvements in land use and investment in developing land.

WOMEN IN FORMAL EMPLOYMENT

Western education has provided opportunities for women to be educated, hence qualifying in various areas of specialization according to the individual's interest. Unlike in the past decades, where women were seen in professions such as teaching and nursing, today women have specialized in areas such as law, administration, medicine, engineering, natural science, regional planning, and the environment.

The woman as her male counterpart is employed to work in the civil service as a lawyer, medical officer, engineer, and administrator. Her gender does not determine the amount of work she can do but her specialization. It is worth mentioning that women in recent times have attained high positions through hard work. In Nigeria, for instance, women have attained positions such as Director Generals, Executive Secretaries, and Directors in various ministries, parastatals, and departments. Their competence cannot in any way be rated below their male counterparts as are clearly manifested in the works of the famous Professor Dora Akunyili, the Director General of the NAFDAC; Dr. Oby Ezekweseli, Education Minister; Dr. Ngozi Okwonjo-Iweala, the former Minister of Finance.

WOMEN IN POLITICS AND GOOD GOVERNANCE

Good governance is a fundamental factor in determining the rate of investment in any region. Women, through their increasing involvement in politics, have spearheaded the fight against corruption, domestic violence, injustice, and the fight for democracy, good governance, and gender equity.

Development is about people and people are at the center of development. For any meaningful development in any country, the people must be at the center of it. Women politicians in Nigeria have distinguished and exhibited a high sense of commitment and humor and have excelled in their political careers. The likes of Hajia Inna Ciroma, Minister of Women Affairs, have made giant strides in their career as politicians toward the upliftment of Nigerian women, though this does not imply that they do not have problems. We have women who have distinguished themselves by contributing to the economic and political development of Nigeria as members of the national and state executive councils, Legislators, Local government councils, councilors, and so on. However, there is still much to be done in the area of women involvement in policy and decision making of the nation.

OBSTACLES TO WOMEN IN DEVELOPMENT

Notwithstanding the apparent contribution of women in the development of our society, there still exist factors militating against their achievements, some of which are:

1. *Indolence.* This is the habit of a total abstinence by women from any public issues, perhaps due to the fear of molestation by the male folk. So if women are not deliberately staying out of work, will you call that indolence on their part?
2. *Low level of education.* This is a great hindrance to a woman's discovery of her ability and competence. A woman's level of education determines the extent to which she can contribute to the development of the country. Most Nigerian women entrepreneurs have limited education; the majorities have secondary or less education, while most traders have no education at all. As a result, they find it difficult to comprehend all the documentations and processes required to obtain loans.
3. *Lack of family planning.* This is the practice whereby a woman is only put to use as a child-producing machine without reasonable spacing to allow her to engage in any economic activity gearing toward the improvement of her family. This can also lead to a population explosion, thereby reducing the life expectancy of women. Can this be linked to the level of education?
4. *Discrimination.* This is the practice of giving preferences to men when it comes to employment/appointment opportunities. This practice is very common in the private sector, which is profit oriented.
5. *Access to capital.* Available studies and life experiences of women entrepreneurs shows that it is very difficult for them to access capital for startup or expansion of their businesses. Some women entrepre-

neurs complained that it is difficult to obtain loans from banks due to lack of collateral, which they always demand.

6. *Limited skills.* A majority of women entrepreneurs have limited occupational skills, apart from those who have been apprenticed as tailors, hairdressers, and so on, most women go into business without any skills, having little knowledge of management practices, accounting, marketing, etc., and operating by trail and error.

7. *Jack-of-all trades approach to business.* Many women entrepreneurs tend to undertake so many activities at the same time or diversify before they have consolidated one business idea. The result is that they dissipate their energies trying to do many things simultaneously, instead of concentrating on building up one enterprise into a medium-scale and successful enterprise. This poses a strain on their managerial capacities.

In addressing the above-mentioned problems, the government of Nigeria has through legislations recognized the dignity of women and prohibited any sort of discrimination, thus giving women the same unlimited opportunities as their male counterparts. It has also put in place programs such as the National Poverty Eradication Program (NAPEP), which provides small- and medium-scale loans to women and the generality of Nigerians for the upliftment of their business and thereby improving their standard of living.

The Women Environmental Program (WEP), in pursuant of its objectives, is making sure the traditional status of women, which was primarily domestic, is elevated to that of a participant in good governance and nation building. In this regard, WEP provides credit loans, training, and other incentives to women to stimulate appropriate economic activities across the strata of the society toward raising the level of contribution to the development of Nigeria.

RECOMMENDATION

Women entrepreneurs should adopt some middle position in their management approach so that their employees feel happy to work for them. They should be firm and decisive and adopt a business-like approach so that their workers, bankers, and customers take them seriously. They should be "professional" managers, combining firmness from the battle-axe approach, with the conciliatory approach of the feminine style, to yield effective leadership of employees. Neither of the extreme approaches leads to high productivity among subordinates. Extreme feminism, which is often accompanied by difference, ambivalence, and weak leadership, dose not yield high productivity.

CONCLUSION

Women have been socialized to be helpmates, to be subservient to men, and not to take on decision making over men. This social conditioning affects the way many women entrepreneurs run their businesses. They lack the drive and motivation to run large, successful companies. They are content with running small enterprises, which they can manage by themselves and just cover costs and little profit. Women entrepreneurs need to borrow from their counterparts in the advanced countries who are running multi-million-dollar manufacturing, retail, and service enterprises.

To become better managers of their businesses, women on their own part should avail themselves of opportunities for management and entrepreneurship development training to acquire business literacy and management skills. In addition, they should learn to utilize the services of business consultants, lawyers, and other professionals. The government, on its own part, should make every effort to improve infrastructure and the business environment, including access to cheap capital, which can bring down the high cost of doing business in Nigeria. Financial institutions should also be more willing to support women entrepreneurs with funds and other technical services.

To the very many women entrepreneurs that I have had discussions with, especially Monica Denis and Patricia Aondakaa, just to mention a couple, and to Scovia Asiimwe and John Ogbodo, I say a big thank you for your contributions.

REFERENCES

Agric Digest, September 15, 2006

Heyzer, N. (2004). *Gender, peace, and disarmament. Disarmament Forum: Women, men, peace, and security.* Available at http://www.unidir.org/pdf/articles/pdf-art1993.pdf.

Kay, G. (1979). *The economic theory of the working class.* London: Macmillan.

PENGASSAN News, 5, No. 1, December 1989

Savheko, P. (1987). *What is labour?* Moscow: Progress.

Sodipo, H. A. (1992). *Dynasty of the missioners* Lagos: Spectum.

The Daily Times. The Nigerian mother. April 6, 2006.

United Nations. (2005). *Women, work, and poverty.* Available at http://www.un-ngls.org/women-2005.pdf

UNAIDS. (2004). *Report on the global AIDS epidemic.* Available at http://www.unaids.org/bangkok2004/GAR2004_html/ExecSummary_en/Execsumm_en.pdf.

Women Entrepreneurs' Resource Book, Providing Women with Business Information, UNIFEM, Lagos, September 2003.

CHAPTER 7

WOMEN ENTREPRENEURS
AND MANAGERS IN SERBIA

Mirjana Radović Marković[1]

Serbian culture is macho culture
And lacks its feminine side

—Adizes

INTRODUCTION

Serbia, like most of the eastern European countries that are in the process
of transition, has appeared in terms of the development of entrepreneurship, especially for the women entrepreneurship. Small or micro businesses became an important factor of growth and employment in these
countries, although these potentials had not been completely used. This
unusual possibility has especially related to those women who, despite their
high education and high participation in the labor market, became entrepreneurs twice as less as men. This difference can be noticed in all countries, regardless of the degree of participation of small or micro businesses
in their economies.

The transition period through which economies of many countries go
greatly reflected on the loss of job safety, which was considered the greatest
achievement of socialist and nonmarket economies. Instead, market move-

The Perspective of Women's Entrepreneurship in the Age of Globalization, pages 77–85
Copyright © 2007 by Information Age Publishing
All rights of reproduction in any form reserved.

ments on the labor market during the 1990s, influenced many people to lose their jobs not only as technological surplus, but also above all as economical surplus. At the same time, the job opportunities decreased, which was primarily reflected in the women's workforce.

The unemployment rate of women was lower in Hungary and Slovenia compared to men, but was higher in Czech Republic, Slovakia, and Romania. This was confirmed in recent data ("Economic Survey of Europe," 2002). The high unemployment rate is in southeastern Europe, like Bosnia and Herzegovina and Macedonia (40%) and Croatia and Yugoslavia (between 22 and 26%).

The asymmetries between the sexes can be noticed in sacking workers, sector employment changes, and opening of new jobs in the private sector. This could be explained by horizontal and vertical segregation of women's jobs, but also with women's position in these economies in which men's work dominates. Accordingly, for many women, self-employment is the only way for the possibility of getting a paid job. In other words, most of the women decide to be self-employed and to start a micro or small business, primarily because of the fact that this was the only possibility to be employed, while the other reasons are much rarer. For example, like those related to women entrepreneurs in developed market economies (desire for self-proving in business, the need for independence, desire to achieve business ambitions, to fully use spare time and to socialize more, etc.).

In the restructuring process of these economies, the trend of movement of employees from the agricultural and industrial sectors toward the services sector is noticed easily. In addition, the data shows that participation of women in education, health care, and social protection is increasing.

THE DEVELOPMENT OF FEMALE ENTREPRENEURSHIP IN SERBIA

How active women are in terms of their contribution to the overall socio-economic changes of a country can be determined in several ways and by the use of different indexes. Some of the most used indexes are employment of women, their position in political and social decision making, educational level, and "conquest" of new occupations.

Computerization is evident in all business spheres and it signifies the markets of the 1990s also influencing the development of some completely new occupations like webmaster and web designer, occupations related to computer graphics creation, computer games creation, and similar positions in which women also found their place. However, in terms of new occupations, it is not always about new jobs, which appear as a product of fast technological changes and the expansion of computer technology. It is about the "conquest" of some existing occupations that were reserved only for men by women.

Statistical data in from many countries shows that the biggest growth in the women's workforce has been in these occupations during the past decade. This index is far behind in Serbia and Yugoslavia, not only when compared to developed countries but also compared to developing countries. The cause for this relatively low participation of the women's workforce in these occupations and leadership positions, in general, has been determined by many factors. Primarily, by economic and political factors that together influenced the general development of private business structure and the growth of employment in it. Consequently, this reflected on the rate of inclusion of women in entrepreneurial and managerial occupations in Serbia. This can be supported by arguments with official statistical data, which show that in the three-decade period of 1953 until 1983, the employment growth rate in the private sector in Serbia was 2.2%, and according to the *Statistical Almanac of the Republic of Serbia, 2003*, the data was even lower, 0.9%. Before the war in former Yugoslavia, in Serbia only 23,000 women out of 991,000 employed were employed in the private sector (1990 data according to the Republic Statistical Institute, January 1991).

According to the same source, in that period, 26,155 companies were registered in Serbia, among which 17,293 were private. Most of them (7,418) were trading companies (7,418) while 1,519 were in financial and other services. The newest data from 2003 shows that there are 70,178 companies registered in Serbia, which is an increase of 44,023 compared to 1990. In addition, in the overall structure of entrepreneurial companies, men participated with 62.2%, while women participated with 38.8% in 2003.

Contributing to the growth of the total number of registered companies are huge numbers of newly opened small companies (Table 7.1).

Out of the total number of registered companies in 2003 (70,178), 96.2% of them were small companies, 2.9% were medium companies,

TABLE 7.1
The Structure of Companies by Size in Serbia, 2003

Economy	Company size [%]
Total	100
Small	96.2
Medium	2.9
Large	0.9

Source: Statistical Almanac of the Republic of Serbia, 2003.

while the percentage of large companies were insignificant (0.9%). Overall, 49.7% of companies had retail trades, motor vehicle repair, and others, while the processing industry had 22.7%. An important fact is that small companies in Central Serbia realized 74.5% of BNP, while Vojvodina realized 25.5%.

EMPLOYMENT, SELF-EMPLOYMENT, AND UNEMPLOYMENT OF WOMEN IN SERBIA

By comparing the active working population of both men and women, a significant difference can be noticed in terms of employment (Table 7.2). Although the average employment rate is 41.6%, this number varies depending on branches and educational level.

Looking at an overall structure of employees, 24.1% are self-employed (Table 7.3). There is also a significant difference if comparison is made between self-employed men and women. Actually, self-employed men are 31.1%, while women are 14.2%.

Mass unemployment has become the trend in the 1990s, which continued into year 2000 and later. According to the data from October 2004, the unemployment rate was 18.5% in Serbia. This rate was significantly higher for women (22.8%) than for men (18.5%). By comparing unemployed

TABLE 7.2
Active Working Population in Serbia, 2004

	Total		Male		Female	
	000	%	000	%	000	%
Active pop.	3398	100	1896	55.79	1502	44.21
Employed	2734	80.46	1593	46.88	1141	33.58
Unempl	664	19.54	302	8.91	362	10.63

Source: Report No. 83, Republic Statistical Institute, Republic of Serbia, 2005.

TABLE 7.3
Women's and Men's Share in Self-Employment, 2004 (%)

Total		Male		Female	
000	%	000	%	000	%
659	100	496	75.2	163	24.8

Source: Report No. 83, Republic Statistical Institute, Republic of Serbia, 2005.

TABLE 7.4
Structure of Unemployment in Serbia by Sex and Education, October 2003 (%)

Education	Total	Men	Women
No school	0.6	0.4	0.8
Incomplete elementary school	3.0	2.8	2.9
Elementary school	18.3	16.4	19.9
High school	67.5	69.5	65.1
College	5.6	5.5	5.6
Faculties, academies	4.9	4.4	5.4
Masters, PhD	0.2	0.4	0.1

Source: Report No. 83, Republic Statistical Institute, Republic of Serbia, 2005.

women to unemployed men in terms of education, it can be seen that women are now advancing, although this difference is not as drastic as it is in some other countries in transition.

For example, in Russia the women participation rate is 21% in the overall picture of unemployed population with high school education, which is twice as much as unemployed men with the same education (Politova, 2001).

The reasons for such a high unemployment rate are numerous: the decrease in productivity, high inflation that in 1993 was the highest in the world and accordingly the sudden poverty, increase in unemployment, and decrease in living standards. All these made an impact on the female population and worsened their position. The custom is that women wait longer for employment than men and that, by an unwritten rule, in economic, social, and political crises lose their jobs and income source, it is rather simple to find an explanation for the extremely hard position of women, which culminated in the past 10 years. Those women who were left out from the working process in the mentioned circumstances were employed mostly in the least profitable and the least-paid branches of the economy. Often modest family budgets did not allow them to start their own business with their own means or savings, which women mostly use to start new businesses. In addition, society offered no help—there were restricted credits or loans—which reflected on women's inability to realize their undutiful entrepreneurial and managerial skills. Therefore, the majority worked in marginal jobs or in some jobs in government or public companies, which mostly were not managerial jobs.

WHY IS THERE A RELATIVELY LOW PERCENTAGE
OF WOMEN IN MANAGERIAL OR LEADERSHIP POSITIONS
IN SERBIA?

Is what is happening in managerial jobs against or past the desires of women? Are women naturally less interested in power and less possessed with the pleasures and risks that it brings and aware of their avoidance of managerial positions? What is the relation between women's social status and real position in the family? How can conditions in different life spheres influence each other, as women do not wish to be locked in a family, but on the other hand they feel a responsibility to commit completely to it."[2]

Answering some of these questions needs analysis and research, which exceeds the scope of this chapter and deserves a separate study. Therefore, without any need to consider these questions in further detail, it can be said that even though women have been equal to men for a long time, there is still a huge gap between equality of women in our society de iure and de facto. "[There is a] double load on women, her job's work and maternity in every way and household work occupy her so much that she has no time left for expertise and thus for advancing in her career, for taking over managerial position...."[3] Thus, the determining influence on the women's social role has been maternity, socialization of children, and specific family duties. This position influenced forming opinions that women are not interested in advancing at work and to taking over managerial and leading positions in a company, in other words, "anatomy determines women's fate." This stereotype lasted for a long time and was one of the barriers for women to achieve the very top in the business hierarchy. Not being able to adequately promote themselves in business under a great load of family problems both influenced women to be in the gap in permanent conflict between roles in family and in a job. In that continual profit of traditional and cultural inheritance and exposure in professional meaning on jobs, which offer a wide spectrum of possibilities, but which, due to their complexity, need the "whole woman," she found herself in a position in which she cannot affirm in both business and family. "Working woman is forced to make great efforts in order to carry out her role, because woman's needs grow faster than capabilities which society and family offer. Our society, which is in crisis, seems to be more suited with closed family, and family members, except for a woman, prefer traditional roles."[4]

Maintenance of the traditional and patriarchal family model, especially in some parts of Serbia as well as "macho culture" domination, is also making it difficult for women to fight for "men's jobs" as entrepreneur and manager. For these reasons, an adequate family support is needed (both moral and material), but also in macro plan, a wider support from the society through various programs for helping women who decide to engage in this sort of activity. We suggest a foundation of agencies that will have a consulting role and on which women can depend on, from generating business ideas to their operating in practice. That support is also important as a support to the family, because it can create a base and offer security to women in their intention to be independent again and to fulfill their society promotion.

Although the need for strong development of private business is more than important, it still does not develop in such a way to be a function of economic growth of our society. For private economy, in order to grow, a wider action of society is required. Therefore, our country is not being separated anymore from its own entrepreneurial roots, intoxicated by politics and still not focused on matters that are not important for life itself. Instead, it is necessary to turn to world economy, which is the place where nations compete with the whole of their authentic values, which they are able to create. Not long ago, we witnessed another game where our economic elite were not able to communicate with the economic elite of the world. Therefore, in order to establish this communication on equal terms and in order to overcome various forms of backwardness, it is necessary to increase the level of sensitivity to society's needs and its development. Certainly, women's need to prove themselves in those occupations, which, in our culture, are traditionally considered to be men's, in order to measure up to other women in the world by their contribution, which are already active in overall economic flows of society. Maybe they will be the ones to start the "wheel of Serbia's development" and therefore, they should get the right opportunity at the right time.

THE APPEARANCE OF THE FIRST EDUCATED MANAGERS AND ENTREPRENEURS IN SERBIA

Despite the expansion of private companies at the beginning of the 1990s, the structure of private companies has not improved significantly compared to the period before, when the number of persons who are into entrepreneurial and managerial activities significantly increased. Actually, the development of private initiatives in Serbia at the beginning of the last decade of the 20th century has affirmed a justly neglected profession, which was, as in other countries with a socialist economy, considered heresy. Accordingly, until the 1990s, there were no special schools for education for these types of occupations, which reflected in the lack of educated managers and entrepreneurs, between both men and women. "According to some data, 30% of our executives are not academically educated and future development demands educated, capable, thus risk-ready personnel."[5]

Only from the middle of the past decade, the first generations of edu-cated managers begun to surface from formal educational process. Among educated people, there are a high percentage of women who are ready to use their knowledge in practice through starting their own business, or employ in managers' positions in existing companies. Because of those rea-sons, women as carriers of these occupations in our society can be exam-ined only in the second half of the previous decade. It is still early to estimate their contribution in creation of new businesses and in opening space for employment. Namely, because of the war in our country, negative rates of investments, and the huge percentage of workers in the gray econ-omy during nineties, their contribution in general economic and social movements certainly cannot be compared with those women in developed and politically and economically stable countries (see Markovic, 2006).

THE PERSPECTIVES OF WOMEN'S ENTREPRENEURSHIP IN SERBIA

With greater capital income in Serbia and economic support to small com-panies, as well as with conduct of general reforms in economy and society, one can rightfully expect a significant growth rate of private businesses.

In new expected conditions, women businesses will have greater contri-butions than before. In addition, there will be conditions that will enable general improvement of the position of women in society, who have in the country's economic misfortune, in the past decade been in the most impacted society segment. It is also expected that the forming of a number of women organizations and their networking, similar to others around the world, will contribute not only to better connections between women and exchange of experiences and knowledge, but also to create new space for employment. Besides that, micro credits for development of women entre-preneurial activities is also of great importance for increasing self-employ-ment of women and the reduction of their unemployment, which is the trend everywhere in the world, especially in countries in transition and developing countries.

NOTES

1. Results are presented from the Mirjana's research on the Project, Serbia and Europe (EVB 149038), financed by the Ministry of Science of Republic Serbia.
2. "Problems in family, sex equality, and so called 'women matter' in social-ism," Collection of works, Institute for Economic Research, Faculty of Econ-omy, Kragujevac, 1989.

3.   Op. cit., p.383.
4.   Op. cit., p. 364.
5.   Dr. Mirjana Radović, "Prestigious profession," interview in "Politika ekspres," May 10, 1993.

REFERENCES

Boreham, R. (1998). *The three-legged stool.* Toronto: Routledge.
Drucker, P. (1994, September/October). The theory of business. *Harvard Business Review,* pp. 95–104.
Marković, M. R. (1995). "Vodič za uspešan biznis," UMS, Beograd.
Marković, M. R. (2005). Žene i mali biznis—Od ideje do realizacije, Poslovni biro, Beograd.
Marković, M. R. (2006). *Entrepreneurship—Theoretical and practical guide on all aspects for starting up the small business.* Belgrade: Link Group.
Politova, O. (2001). *Women entrepreneurs in the Russian Federation.* USAID.

CHAPTER 8

WOMEN LEADERS

Case Study of Serbia

Mirjana Radović Marković

INTRODUCTION

The battle for women's rights started back in the late 18th century, which set the stage for the rise of women's movements. Women grew increasingly dissatisfied with the limitations society had placed on their activities. The traditional thinking was the common cliché that a woman's place was in the kitchen, and a woman's job was to clean the house, look after the children, and wash the dishes. The current generations of women are definitely more enthusiastic and determined to succeed in their careers, not having to depend on their male counterparts. Women are not only becoming the backbone of families but also the backbone of several companies. The new cliché might be "in a successful company there is always a woman responsible." Women have demonstrated that they know how to keep things in order and are great problem solvers. They are hard workers and strive to achieve their goals. These statements might well be used as the definition of an independent, successful woman in the 21st century.

But in spite of their great interest in business and careers, the advancement in their abilities to think and decide for themselves, and most impor-

The Perspective of Women's Entrepreneurship in the Age of Globalization, pages 87–94
Copyright © 2007 by Information Age Publishing
All rights of reproduction in any form reserved.

tantly to make their own decisions (unlike before), women continue to face a "boardroom barrier." Recent research from the Leader's Edge in Philadelphia suggests that external factors hamper women as they strive for executive positions. The research has showed that "professional women are proactive in advancing their careers, but the majority believe that their corporation's culture—factors outside their direct control—excludes women from the higher echelons of power and that a board-room barrier exists within their companies" (M. Shepard, principal of The Leader's Edge, personal communication). For the purpose of the research, "boardroom barrier" was defined as "those factors external to women that prevent them, and not their male counterparts, from moving to the top of their organizations."

There is widespread belief that the old "glass ceiling" has been cracked, with large numbers of women in business and middle management. In spite of advancements, this glass ceiling is not completely removed. There are still many companies that do not acknowledge that women can do just as good a job as men and there are many limiting sexist and chauvinistic views on women running certain businesses.

All women experience barriers and there are internal and external bar-riers to overcome. Gregory (1999) stated that internal barriers are based on both perceptions of one's capability to work in a leadership role and personal leadership styles. External barriers are described as barriers that an individual has no control over, such as lack of resources and not being included in collaborative projects. According to the research on the "boardroom barrier," "Two-thirds of women say they desire top-level execu-tive positions, and more than half of the women surveyed will move to another company if they are passed over for promotion, suggesting serious implications both for ambitious women and for their companies."

The right to equality and nondiscrimination based on gender is increas-ingly recognized as being at the core of workers' rights and human rights activities. Gender equality in employment is provided for in various inter-national human rights instruments, including the Universal Declaration of Human Rights, the UN Convention on the Elimination of All Forms of Dis-crimination Against Women, the ILO Discrimination (Employment and Occupation) Convention, 1958 (No. 111), the Equal Remuneration Con-vention, 1951 (No. 100), the Workers with Family Responsibilities Conven-tion, 1981 (No. 156), and the ILO Declaration on Fundamental Principles and Rights at Work. These have affirmed the importance of the rights-based approach to gender equality, but stressed that operationalization of the approach in terms of practical policies and programs are still a chal-lenge. But in spite of unequal pay, discrimination, and stereotypes there has never been a better time for women in the business world.

SEX-ROLES AND LEADERSHIP

Leadership is based on two words, "pressure and support" and that the leadership is the power to influence people to move in a direction that you believe in your heart is a good direction for most people" (Fennell, 1999, p. 267). Adams and Yoder (2001) noted, "Evidence from contemporary studies on sex-roles and leadership indicates that men and women, with similar education, career aspirations and training, have basically identical scores on measures of psychological masculinity and femininity" (p. 45). In other words, the traits assumed to be important in good leadership are found among people of both genders.

What makes a leader is a complex question. It includes factors from the environment in which an individual was raised, his or her family situation, and his or her personality traits. The following discussion is a summary of the author's observations plus some of the conclusions of others.

According to an overview of research conducted by the author, women are a fast-growing segment of the business community worldwide. The leadership characteristics required to make a success in this new reality are very much "feminine characteristics." These characteristics include:

1. self-confidence, an independent mindset, and a willingness to take risks
2. ability to balance work and family (most are married)
3. age from 40 to 60 years old
4. well educated with skills in management and entrepreneurship
5. integration of personal and professional
6. intuition
7. social skills
8. direction
9. hires competent, trustworthy people (not putting priority on loyalty)
10. see communication and conflict resolution as key to organizational success
11. men and women tend to lead in different ways, namely, women leadership strategy is based on family patterns; it means that women tend to view solving problems differently than men, women tend to be more holistic in their thinking
12. leaders must be conscious of what is perceived by others and develop strategies that are proactive in building success; Marcano (1997) described this as "know thyself" and further stated that it is important to be honest and objective when evaluating your strengths and abilities as well as your goals

13. continual professional growth
14. leaders need to have a clear sense of their own vision and beliefs
15. they orchestrate a web of relationships inside and outside their companies, which foster a feeling of inclusion and allows the free exchange of information necessary for organizational effectiveness
16. women are naturally better at nurturing and making people feel connected: "They create communities rather than mechanical hierarchies"

RESEARCH: CASE STUDY OF SERBIA

Much has been written about the glass ceiling, the double standard, and other barriers to women in business. As we can conclude, earlier women do not have a problem developing an effective leadership style. What they do struggle with more than men, however, is claiming the authority to lead and to trust them. With more trust, the gender gap at the workplace could be significantly reduced and women will contribute more as leaders and managers.

In this research, we tried to measure the role of women leaders in the Serbian business community and to define the barriers to women's career advancement. We asked respondents the following questions: What do you think about women leaders? Do you trust women leaders? Could they be equally as successful as men in the business world?

Methodology

- Interviews conducted from 1,476 people: 726 women and 750 men
- Interviewees were individuals between 18 and 60 years of age
- Approximately 30% of the respondents were business owners
- 73% were married, 19% single, and 8% divorced

Key Findings

- The barriers to womens' advancement in business are remarkably similar across the Balkan region and the biggest cities in Serbia: Belgrade, Novi Sad, and Nis.
- The majority (63%) of women respondents trust women leaders and most of them prefer to work in some firm where a woman is the

leader or executive manager. In addition, they believe that women want to reach the top, and are equally as ambitious as men.

- Most respondents (60%) say that corporate culture is the most significant barrier to women achieving top executive positions, while only 29% think work/family balance is a significant barrier to advancement, and 36% believe that a lack of self-promotion holds women back from achieving top-level positions
- A majority of the men questioned had a negative attitude toward women executives. They expressed stereotypes and preconceptions about women's roles and abilities in business. The men stressed that women have a lack of general management experience, lack of skills and knowledge, and lack of role models. Male respondents gave the following specific replies related to our questions:
  - "We are here in the Balkan and we argue for a traditional model of society."
  - "Women have been fighting for equal rights for nearly all of the time and now that they have it they expect special treatment because they are females."
  - "I do not trust women in business and I do not accept them seriously."
  - "I am afraid of those women."
  - "I hate feminist community and culture."
  - "Women must stay at home and be leaders in their families but not in the business world. The leadership position in business is reserved for men."
  - "Women leaders are actually men dressed like women."

It is very interesting that a great number of men do not make a difference between women leaders and women feminists, who are not very popular in this region. In addition, about 20% of women respondents in the research share the opinions of the men.

About 10% of men respondents are afraid of women domination in the business world because it could change the natural balance between women and men and decrease the traditional role of men in society and family. Therefore, they would not like domination by businesspersons.

Among young women (ages 18–35) exist the greatest interest for leadership and entrepreneurship. Increasingly, they are exploring opportunities to reach their professional goals and expressed their opinions with the following words:

1. Female leaders have more of a struggle because they are females and no one will take them seriously so they have to push and make themselves known to the world and allow the world to see their capabili-

ties while male owners don't have to worry about the struggle of fitting in and trying to live and work up to society's standards. Because they are men they already have the "macho man" persona and the alter ego that men have.

2. Women have to fight harder and be stronger if they want to live and work in a man's world. You have to adapt to the surroundings. Don't expect a man to be a gentleman and hold the door open for you, don't expect him to do anything out of the ordinary that a man would do for a female because in a sense you should be getting treated like his fellow counterparts and not expect differently. In order to fit in with the men you have to in a sense think, work, and act like them, meaning don't think that they will treat you like the female you are. You have to be strong—not every man that you encounter will treat you like this but in order to show off your strengths you should expect this.

3. It is obvious that women have come a long way as successful professionals. Life in the workplace has become much more diversified as an increased number of women have made their presence felt in many industries and professions. The female task force has expanded with exponential strength, and thus has its dire importance in the professional world. Whether they like it or not, men have to accept, finally, those women are marching up the corporate ladder confidently, full speed ahead.

4. Women used to be much more "quiet and passive" in the workplace due to the relatively small number of female employees in comparison to males. Women today, on the other hand, have begun assuming their positions by using all their God-given powers of intelligence and organization. Warren Farrell, author of *Why Men Are the Way They Are,* explains that men are jealous of the "beauty power" that allows women to get certain things based on their physical assets. Perhaps it is less that women use their beauty and more likely that men judge them based on their physical beauty.

5. The reasons that people start and lead business among women is to bring in and focus on a clientèle of mainly women. Most times women start businesses that deal with products that women use, such as clothes, makeup, and home products. The most successful companies run by women are those that use women's special skills. These special skills are style, fiscal sense, and public relations. Their strengths as business owners are their public relations and the clientèle they bring in. Their weakness as business owners is overcoming the sexism that exists. Their biggest fear is finding clientèle that

will do business with a woman. I think these men feel this way because they are insecure.

6. I simply think that women just became even smarter. Speaking from a personal point of view, I know that being happy and successful are very important to me. They go hand in hand. Most of the women I know feel the same way. I believe that as the years progress, women will be involved in an even bigger part of the economy, because young girls are going to follow their female role models.

7. I also feel that some high positions are better suited to women because men have humongous ego problems.

8. I personally think that women can do whatever men do—sometimes better. There have always been glass ceilings for women in the workforce. However, many women are getting closer to this ceiling and some of them have at least attempted to break through this ceiling. The reason why many people think that women are not capable of being in the workforce is because of the connotation that "women should stay home and take care of the home."

FINAL CONCLUSION

In conclusion, it can be said that women are now much more motivated and ready to reach their professional dreams and be leaders, not only in the Serbia and Balkan regions but all over the world, than they were before. Until recently, leadership was considered by many to be the last bastion of male dominance in the business world. This is no longer true. More businesses are now being started by women than are being started by men. However, there are still a lot of men who don't think women should be in these positions and hold no respect for them at all. As time goes on, women are going to form a bigger and bigger part of the business world, and these men are just going to have to accept it and face the reality, because no matter what they feel and how much they are against it, the world is changing and this is going to happen regardless of how they feel.

REFERENCES

Adams, J., & Yoder, J. D. (1985). *Effective leadership for women and men.* Norwood, NJ: Ablex.

Blackmore, J. (1989). Educational leadership: A feminist critique and reconstruction. In J. Smyth (Ed.), *Critical perspective on educational leadership* (pp. 93–130). London: Falmer Press.

Bogdan, R., & Biklen, S. (1998). *Qualitative research for education: An introduction to theory and methods* (3rd ed.). Boston: Allyn & Bacon.

Calabrese, R. L., Short, G. S., & Zepeda, S. J. (1996). *Hands-on leadership tools for principals.* New York: Eye on Education.

Cowley, W. H. (1928, April). Three distinctions in the study of leaders. *Journal of Abnormal and Social Psychology,* pp. 144–157.

Fennell, H. A. (1999). Feminine faces of leadership: Beyond structural-functionalism. *Journal of School Leadership, 9,* 255–285.

Freeman, W. B. (1996). *God,s little instruction book on character* (6th ed.). Tulsa, OK: Honor Books.

Gorton, R. A., & Snowden, P. E. (1993). *School leadership and administration* (5th ed.). Dubuque, IA: Brown & Benchmark.

Hagberg Consulting Group. (1998). Females and leadership (Document No. 98). Available at http//www.leadership.development.com

Johnson, R. B. (1999). *Cases in qualitative research.* Los Angeles, CA: Pyrczak Publishing.

Lipham, J. M. (1964). Leadership and administration in behavioral science and educational administration. In *Yearbook of the National Society for the Study of Education* (pp. 119–141). Chicago: University of Chicago Press.

Marcano, R. (1997). Gender, culture, and language in school administration: Another glass ceiling for Hispanic women. *Advancing Women in Leadership Journal, 1*(1), 1–8.

Marković, M. R. (2006). *Entrepreneurship—Theoretical and practical guide on all aspects for starting up small business.* Belgrade: Link Group.

Radovic, M. (2005). Women and small business. "Poslovni biro," Belgrade.

CHAPTER 9

LEADING WOMEN ENTREPRENEURS OF THAILAND

Siri Terjesen, Caroline Hatcher, Tatiana Wysocki, and Jessica Pham

Marriage is like an elephant—the husband is the front legs that choose the direction, the wife the back legs, providing the power!

—Thai legend

INTRODUCTION

The Thai legend above illustrates the important yet veiled role of women in Thai society. Women comprise 46% of the labor force; 26% of senior officials, legislators, and managers (UNDP, 2006); and nearly 50% of entrepreneurs (Minniti, Allen, & Langowitz, 2006) in Thailand. Most of these women are running small companies, but a handful head large, growth-oriented entrepreneurial firms. In this chapter, we profile four leading Thai women who have been recognized with the highly prestigious "Leading Women Entrepreneurs of the World" (LWEW) award: Kobkarn Wattanavranangkul, Khungying Pornthip Narongdej, Supapan Pichaironarongsongkram, and Supaluck Umpujh.

The Perspective of Women's Entrepreneurship in the Age of Globalization, pages 95–108
Copyright © 2007 by Information Age Publishing
All rights of reproduction in any form reserved.

Despite the awareness of female entrepreneurs' role in economic development (OECD, 2000), there has been limited academic attention (Baker, Aldrich, & Liou, 1997; de Bruin, Brush, & Welter, 2006), particularly to highly successful "gazelle" entrepreneurs. Extant female entrepreneurship research has explored a range of topics including gender differences (e.g., Birley, 1989; Hisrish & Brush, 1984), performance (e.g., Fasci & Valdez, 1998), and financing (e.g., O'Gorman & Terjesen, 2005). Researchers have called for studies of entrepreneurship that take into account the role of culture (Hayton, George, & Zahra, 2002) and are of a qualitative nature (Davidsson, 2004; Gartner & Birley, 2002).

This chapter proceeds as follows. We begin by providing an overview of enterprise and female entrepreneurship in Thailand. Next, we describe relational theory in the context of female entrepreneurship, paying particular attention to the role of family. Following a description of the data and methodology, we review four case studies of Thai "gazelle" entrepreneurs. Following a discussion of key themes, we conclude with implications and suggestions for future research.

NATIONAL CONTEXT: THAILAND

Entrepreneurship in Thailand

Since 1999, the annual Global Entrepreneurship Monitor (GEM) study has examined the prevalence rates of entrepreneurial activity in over 40 countries around the world. Each year, an adult population survey is conducted by telephone or face-to-face with at least 2,000 individuals, and is designed to yield a representative sample of the population within each country. A consistent finding in the GEM data is the extremely high prevalence of entrepreneurship among Thai adults (Minniti et al., 2006), and notably the nearly equal ratio of men and women. Figure 9.1 depicts the total entrepreneurial activity for 32 countries participating in the GEM study in 2005. Approximately 19% of Thai women and 22% of Thai men reported that they are in the process of starting a business, currently own or manage a firm, or are undertaking some entrepreneurial initiatives in an existing firm. This equates to an estimated 8.1 million adults in Thailand.

The high rate of entrepreneurial activity has been attributed to a number of factors including government policies, positive perceptions of entrepreneurship (Virasa et al., 2006), and the Buddhist religion (Dana, 2006). Thailand has a free-market culture and entrepreneurs make substantial contributions to growing the Thai economy (Dana, 2006). The government of Thailand has undertaken a series of National Economic Development Plans encouraging the development of entrepreneurship and

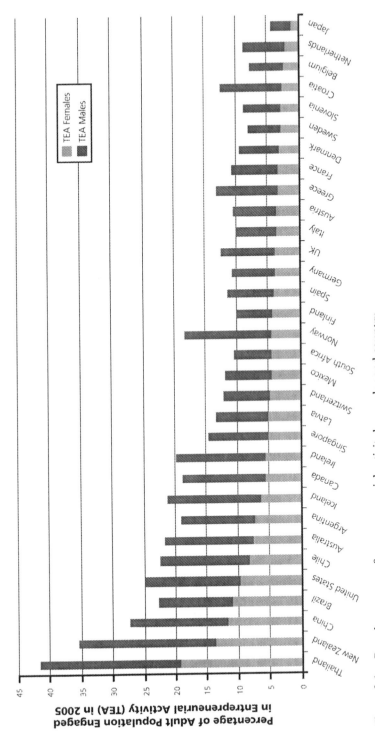

Figure 9.1. Prevalence rates of entrepreneurial activity by gender and country.
Source: Minniti et al. (2006) GEM Report.

97

enterprise (Dana, 2006), as well as the role of women, such as the Long-Term Women's Development Plan. Over 95% of the Thai population is Buddhist. The Buddhist religion encourages all of its followers, regardless of gender, education, occupation, age, or social status, to follow the Buddha's teachings (dhamma) to obtain enlightenment. There are seven qualities of Buddhism that are compatible with entrepreneurship: asceticism, self-reliance, taking initiative, love of work, diligence, patience, and frugality and efficiency (Dana, 2006).

ROLE OF WOMEN IN THAI SOCIETY

There have been a number of studies profiling the role of women in the Thailand labor force. While, in the 1940s, women were rarely found in the business world (Siengthai & Leelakulthanit, 1993), women now play a substantial role. According to Lawler (1996, p. 154), "Rapid growth and modernization have generated pressures for change in recent years." Indeed, Thailand has one of the most favorable situations for women in Asia (ILO, 2006). A substantial part of Thailand's recent annual growth rates (7–8%) is due to the expansion of the service, manufacturing, and tourism sectors, in which women play a large role. In villages, Thai women have "occupational multiplicity" and, in addition to domestic work, paid and unpaid work will often fulfill important trading roles, for example selling surplus rice and vegetables from the farm (Coyle & Kwang, 2000).

Females in Thailand tend to have more positive attitudes toward entrepreneurship than do their male counterparts. The GEM Thailand study reported that women are more likely to know entrepreneurs, perceive entrepreneurial opportunities, and believe that entrepreneurship is a good career choice. See Table 9.1.

Female entrepreneurship in Thailand has a strong family component, with over 70% of enterprises involving other family members (Viravan, 1998). While most women-led businesses in Thailand are in cottage industries, many are corporations (36%) and a few are even listed on the stock exchange (1.4%) (Viravan, 1998). Women are at the helm of some of the largest firms in the hotel, manufacturing, boating, technology, shopping center, and restaurant industries. In this chapter, we profile four of these women. The Asian Financial crisis in 1997 actually helped many Thai women break through the glass ceilings of senior management, as these Thai women were resilient throughout the crisis (Viravan, 1998). During the crisis, the women-led firms tried to help their staff. Of the women-led firms, 77% refused to lay off workers, 78% refused to introduce salary cutoffs for staff, and 92% refused to force their staff to take a vacation leave (Viravan, 1998).

TABLE 9.1
Thai Attitudes toward Entrepreneurship

Percentage of the Adult Population Agreeing	Male	Female
Know someone who started a business in the past 2 years	43.0%	57.0%
Perceive good startup opportunities	40.3%	59.7%
Fear of failure prevents startup	35.1%	64.9%
Have knowledge and skills to start a company	46.1%	61.0%
Entrepreneurship is a good career choice	39.2%	60.8%
Successful own business is high status	39.3%	60.7%
Lots of media coverage for successful entrepreneurs	39.1%	60.9%

Source: Virasa et al. (2006) Thailand GEM report.

BACKGROUND: FEMALE ENTREPRENEURSHIP, RELATIONSHIPS, AND CULTURE

There is a growing body of research on female entrepreneurs. Some of this work focuses on a range of economic factors associated with national-level variations in female entrepreneurial activity, such as unemployment rates and economic freedom indices (e.g., Minniti & Nardone, 2007). These factors may not fully explain the gender patterns observed, particularly as women have been found to be more sensitive to noneconomic determinants of entrepreneurship (Minniti et al., 2006). We briefly highlight three salient themes in extant research: the role of family, relationships, and culture.

Brush (1992) describes women's entrepreneurship as an integrated network and focused on relationships. Relational theory (Miller, 1976) describes how women's sense of self and personal development is shaped by relationships with others, particularly family members. From their early childhoods, girls are more likely to see themselves as similar to their mothers, who are focused on relationships. In contrast, boys grow up seeking autonomy from their mothers (Chodorow, 1978). Subsequently, women devote large proportions of their lives caring for others. Relational theory is particularly salient to female entrepreneurs' experiences and approaches (Buttner, 2001). Female entrepreneurs frequently report the presence and importance of networks to others, particularly kin (e.g., Renzulli, 1998). While these gender patterns have some universal application, cultural values also play a part in the performance of gender. Thai gender roles are strongly influenced by the values of harmony, politeness, and a worldview based on the metaphor of *jai*, the Thai word for *heart*. Unlike

Western Aristotelian conceptions of the separation of heart and mind, Thais are much more interested in relationships and social harmony and the word *jai* includes both heart and mind (Knutson, 2004; Komin, 1991).

METHODOLOGY AND DATA

Entrepreneurship is a young scholarly field, characterized by heterogeneous phenomenon requiring closeup analysis (Davidsson, 2004). Qualitative methodologies in entrepreneurship enable researchers to observe (Davidsson, 2004) and generate unique insights (e.g., Aldrich, 1992; Gartner & Birley, 2002). The four Thai women profiled in this chapter were identified based on their membership in LWEW, and are part of a larger ongoing study. Women nominated to LWEW must be current or past owners of public or private firms with annual sales of at least US$20 million in developed countries (or US$5 million in developing countries) and identified as role models for their civic and charitable activities. The chapter is based on (1) participant observations and informal interviews during the LWEW conference in Bangkok, Thailand, in March 2006; (2) semi-structured in-depth life history interviews (each 90–120 minutes long) conducted in November 2006; (3) on-site visits to three of the four organizations; and (4) media coverage of the entrepreneurs and their firms. We analyzed the material, following categorization and subcategorization methods suggested by Strauss and Corbin (1990). By collecting data from multiple sources, these exploratory case studies probe the ways in which successful Thai female entrepreneurs articulate their experiences.

CASE STUDIES

Kobkarn Wattanavranangkul is Chairperson of Toshiba Thailand, one of the few remaining Thai–Japanese joint ventures. Having followed her parents into business, Kobkarn exemplifies the Thai values of family, continuity, and social responsibility to both her family and her nation. She described the vision of equality in her family:

> Ever since my brothers and I were young, we have seen the way our parents were working together. My father was like the pioneer...he always had a vision what to do...he is the engineer. But my mother...she is the management side...the logistical part, the financial part. It was always an equal partnership between my parents...and between the Thai partners and the Japanese partners.

Kobkarn's ideas about equality persist today in the way she thinks about and runs her firm,

> I have never had the issue of gender...to me...we have never thought that...I mean...we are women...or we are men or who is better than whom...But we are thinking that everyone is equally important...it's what you can contribute, it's what is inside you that you can do for the others. To us that is very important. So, regardless of gender, regardless of nationalities, regardless of age, regardless of education background, of family background...we feel that everyone...is equally as important as one red brick...the president, the chairperson like myself, or even my driver, or just the normal staff or the labor—no one is more than one brick and no one is less than one brick. Every position is equally important...and the duty of the leader like us...we have to make sure and we have to plan which brick will be...will be placed in what position. And everyone should join and create a good architecture together.

Kobkarn sees her role as CEO as one of a partnership, with business, family, and society. She reports striving for a respectful and caring relationship with her staff, a commitment to the vendors who sell her Toshiba products, and support for the broader community, including active support of educational projects in prisons and environmental projects to help the December 2004 tsunami victims. Kobkarn attributes the success to her staff and the values her mother taught her:

> My mother always taught me that human beings are the most valuable resources, and also the most sensitive. Nobody is perfect, I am aware of that. The question is how to make the most out of one's good side.

Kobkarn's driving metaphor for life highlights the Thai way of thinking about entrepreneurship, which ties personal opportunity to responsibility to others. For her, business success is built on connecting staff and vendors in the enterprise of nation-building,

> To me, achievement is to be the role model of the others, to contribute to the society and I hope that I can be like light...light meaning that I can give light to the others...and at the same time light meaning that you need...to have burning energy to go forward, burning energy to work harder, burning energy to be able to give something for the others...so it's not only to conquer things but maybe to conquer something in order to give...so giving is more important than conquering... but you do need to conquer.

Khungying Pornthip Narongdej began her career at the age of 17 as a secretarial assistant to her father's business, Siam Motors Company. She built a high level of understanding of the automotive assembly business and later introduced new innovations in the company's Public Relations and Human Resource departments, again under the watchful eye of her father. When Khungying Pornthip married Dr. Kasem Narongdej in 1969, her father presented them with the Siam Yamaha Company as a wedding gift. Under Khungying Pornthip's guidance and vision, the company won the rights to become the first Yahama motorcycle manufacturer outside of Japan.

Sensing the conservatism and different priorities of her clan about the importance of people in the organization, Khungying Pornthip left the Siam Motors Group to become President and CEO of local conglomerate, KPN Group. KPN has diverse business interests, including manufacturing and a national music academy. Although she has been hailed as the leading industrialist in Thailand (Tatler, 2006), she proudly also suggests that her image as mother is just as important,

> You know a lot of Thai children I will say, more than half a million, call me Mother. They start calling Mummy too, like my sons. When I treated them like my kids, they are going to feel like they're my kids. So they always call "May-ying." [In Thai, *may* is mother, *ying* is lady.]

Khungying Pornthip reports balancing this image of a tough businesswoman and mother, both in the family and as a brand, very delicately,

> But I did very work on it and so far, I'm one of the role models in that I have made it work in the marriage and personal life and public life, you know— my career. And in Thailand, you know, I think my journey has a lot to do with culture. And history. We have a lot of sayings in Thai that date back centuries, including that a marriage is like an elephant. The husband is the front legs, and the wife is the hind legs. I always show high respect for my husband and always he is still the chairman, I am just the chairman's wife. And he says the real chairman is me. But I still pretend...I'm being very humble. And I think a lot of my journey to success is because of my humility. I see people as a key factor of life. In daily life, in business life, if you don't have good relationships...you get nowhere.

She further explains this blend of mastery and femininity by sharing some Thai history,

> In Thailand, the King actually has to go out in front on the elephants and duel...and in a lot of cases, the King gets killed. But the Queen is the one who has to continue and fight and will not continue the war, so a lot of them win the war or get their kingdoms back through their wives. Historically, Thai women have had strong recognition.

The image of the strong woman continues, and Khungying Pornthip elaborates that Thai women at home "rock the cradle, take care of the babies, bring up the family, do the cooking, schooling, and welfare, and at the same time, in the time of war, they also can be at the battlefield and save the nation, the little kingdoms that Thailand is made of." This historical balancing act between wife and husband provides a complex challenge for such an entrepreneur who sees herself as a mixture of "fairy godmother" in the music industry, one who has made "a lot of them rich and famous" and a "very tough businesswoman" in the industrial world. When you go to her [Khungying referring to herself], "it pays to have done your work well, she's very tough. She always smiles, she always laughs, but she's very tough."

Supapan Pichaironarongsongkram is the third-generation woman owner and operator of Supatra Chao Phraya Express Boat ferry crossing services on Bangkok's Chao Phraya River. She has served as Managing Director since 1971 and Chairman since 1998, and has expanded her business interests to include the Supatra restaurants and the Supatra Hua Hin Resort. Supapan describes how, in Thai families, the eldest is always expected to take over the business but that women in particular learn their responsibility when they are very young:

> For women, there is a lot more responsibilities because they [parents] expect a lot more. If you have young boys, if they are rich, they would have a kind of swinging life. Daughters would never have that kind of life. So they will be more attentive to the business immediately after they finish school. We cannot experiment with our lives because we know what is waiting. It's almost like, you know, a duty to come back to. We're taught that way. It's all being absorbed in the bloodstream as you grow up. In the school yard, you are always taught to show gratitude. Gratitude is a big thing in Asia. And you have to be persistent to show that it's gratifying for them to raise you.

Supapan also believes that Thai women succeed because they proceed very gently and can work with and around men because

> There isn't great expectations for women to succeed...men do accept women...because in a way we are not a threat to them; we are more like a partner and we are more like the motherly figure to them. I think you will find all of us again, gentle. We don't look aggressive. I've seen many Americans who look very aggressive...you know, I'm very glad I don't work with them; but they are different...you look at Thai women and we are not like that. We are very silent. We are very calm...But when you look at us in business; you'd be surprised. And you think, "Is that really her?"

She considers her sense of self to be based on her role in society, rather than her role as CEO:

I think we are very simple. We don't talk about success; we don't talk about how much we earn. And our success...I don't think we don't even look at ourselves as being successful...I think I have achieved something in life. And I have been very useful to society. I have served the public. We carry something like 70,000 passengers per day, and that's a lot of work. Yes. So I think that's work, and we bring them home safely. I mean, that's our duty.

Supaluck Umpujh, Executive Vice President and Vice Chairperson of the US$580 million retail empire Thai Mall Group Company, owns and runs the most popular group of shopping complexes in Thailand. As the eldest daughter of founder Supachai Umpujh, Supaluck runs the business with the help of her six brothers and sisters, and is responsible for marketing and new project development. The Thai Mall Group operates seven shopping complexes, with Supaluck's most recent success being the glamorous Siam Paragon Shopping Centre with its stores, restaurants, cinemas, and other attractions in central Bangkok.

Supaluck attributes the firm's success, and especially perseverance in the 1997 financial crisis, to a sense of family and professionalism:

Our company is a family-owned business. 100% family-owned business...but we like to make the company work with professionalism. We like professional work but we are used to taking care of people like our family. So my concept of working is that we treat the staff as a happy family, but you work professionally to be effective and efficient in the business.

Supaluck's strong connection to her now 74-year-old father enabled her to benefit from his wisdom:

I feel that usually the father and the daughter have more connection than the father and the son. Because when they ask you to do things...the daughter kind of obeys and listens, but with the son...there may be some kind of man-to-man conflict...it's not like that for the father trying to give what he thinks to the daughter...which is much easier than to give to the son. Having such a father, you know businessmen, or everyone you know are entrepreneurs.

Her 10,000 employees are intensely "loyal," as she describes:

My company is quite young, just 25 years old...but many staff in senior management have worked here for more than 20 years...because you take care of them like family, and even if people leave our company...they go to big corporations and they come back because they feel like here is more...like a home for them.

This recurring theme of home, family, and connection shapes Supaluck's work ethic and business values. She feels a great sense of responsibility to her organization to work hard and "to show a lot of spirit, give a lot. To go forward all the time, like a fighter." Her leadership and business strategy is based on this people focus,

> I work with total dedication and devotion, and people see how hard you are working, you show that you are a role model...you keep your word and commitment is very important. If you promise this, and then you change, people will not trust or have confidence in you. And confidence and trust is very important.

She suggests that she learned to be a successful entrepreneur by her father's side and values his wisdom,

> My father always says that if you lost your money you can find it any time...but if you lose your trust and honesty...money cannot buy it back. So that's how we treat others and then we can get trust and confidence from our people and then you show your dedication and you treat them well and try to reward them...very important.

Supaluck recalls that *Fortune* magazine described her as a "butterfly", but she proudly characterizes herself as an "iron businesswoman because I work very hard, and very, very hard compared to all the men of my age, and I am quite tough, but not tough in terms of negotiation but tough because of a lot problems of building this 500,000-square-meter shopping center in only 3 years...I can take that." Her business success is built upon her strong sense of the value of acting as a role model and visionary perspective based on the traditional family values of her culture combined with personal tenacity and ambition.

DISCUSSION AND CONCLUSIONS

A woman is like a tea bag. You don't know how strong she is
until you put her in hot water.

As the Thai saying above articulates, the strength and perseverance of women is a major component of Thai culture. Our study has provided unique insight into the experiences of four of the world's leading female entrepreneurs. In the context of Thailand, this research substantiates the role of relationships not only to family, but also to employees, consumers, and society. In our interviews, Kobkarn, Khungying Pornthip, Supapan, and Supaluck extended their descriptions of entrepreneurship and management to encompass relationships with others. Importantly, their conceptualizations and the LWEW event received a lot of attention at home and abroad. Thailand's King Bhumibol Adulyadej served as its patron.

As LWEW Co-Chair, Kobkarn believes that the international significance of the event will enhance opportunities for women even further:

> I see this is a beginning because we have to live up to this. And we would like this to be an opportunity that people will listen to us more... Before my mother received the award when she tried to say something or I tried to say something no one listened... it was very difficult to change things, to improve things, to do good things to the others. But once you've been recognized, especially by an international platform, then people will listen to you more. And this is important. But I say it is beginning because we have to use this opportunity. So I try to be more active. And I believe the other Thai honorees also try to use these opportunities so that we can do more so that people will benefit so that... that kind of thing.

Our study suggests a number of dimensions for future work. Longitudinal career history studies could provide a more nuanced picture of female entrepreneurial careers. As an entrepreneur's social network is one aspect of an integrated entrepreneurial career (Johansson & Monsted 1997), our findings could be extended to research on other types of entrepreneurial participation. For example, individuals with ownership experience are more likely to act as invest informally in others' entrepreneurial ventures (Szerb, Rappai, Makra, & Terjesen 2007).

Finally, the Thailand government's current strategy is to develop the country's knowledge-based society through entrepreneurship and innovation. Entrepreneurship is expected to continue to make large contributions to local and national growth. The government's stated focus on enhancing entrepreneurial education and enabling women may provide the groundwork for future female entrepreneurs.

REFERENCES

Aldrich, H. E. (1992). Methods in our madness? Trends in entrepreneurship research. In D. L. Sexton & J. D. Kasarda (Eds.), *The state of art of entrepreneurship research* (pp. 292–313). Boston: PWS.

Baker, T., Aldrich, H. E., & Liou, N. (1997). "Invisible entrepreneurs: The neglect of women business owners by mass media and scholarly journals in the United States. *Entrepreneurship and Regional Development, 9,* 221–238.

Birley, S. (1989). Female entrepreneurs: Are they really different? *Journal of Small Business Management, 27*(1), 32–37.

Brush, C. G. (1992). Research on women business owners: Past trends, a new perspective and future directions. *Entrepreneurship Theory and Practice, 16*(4), 5–30.

Buttner, E. H. (2001). Examining female entrepreneurs' management style: An application of a relational frame. *Journal of Business Ethics, 29*(3), 253–270.

Chodorow, N. (1978). *The reproduction of mothering.* Berkeley: University of California.

Coyle, S., & J. Kwong. (2000). Women's work and social reproduction in Thailand. *Journal of Contemporary Asia, 30*(4), 492–596.

Dana, L. P. (2007). *"Thailand," Asian models of entrepreneurship: Context, policy and practice.* World Scientific.

Davidsson, P. (2004). *Researching entrepreneurship.* New York: Springer.

de Bruin, A., Brush, C.G., & F. Welter. (2006). Introduction to the special issue: Towards building cumulative knowledge on women's entrepreneurship. *Entrepreneurship Theory and Practice, 30*(5), 585–593.

Fasci, M. A., & Valdez, J. (1998). A performance contrast of male- and female-owned small accounting practices. *Journal of Small Business Management, 36*(3), 1–7.

Gartner, W. B., & Birley, S. (2002). Introduction to the special issue on qualitative methods in entrepreneurship research. *Journal of Business Venturing, 17,* 387–395.

Hayton, J. C., George, G., & Zahra, S. A. (2002). National culture and entrepreneurship: A review of behavior research. *Entrepreneurship Theory and Practice, 26*(4), 33–52.

Hisrich, R. D., & Brush, C. (1984). The woman entrepreneur: Management skills and business problems. *Journal of Small Business Management, 22*(1), 30–37.

International Labor Organization (ILO). (2006). *Yearbook of labor statistics.* Geneva: Author.

Johanisson, B., & Monsted, M. (1997). Contextualising entrepreneurial networking. *International Studies of Management and Organisation, 27*(3), 109–136.

Komin, S. (1991). *Psychology of the Thai people. Values and behavioural patterns.* Bangkok: National Institute of Development Adminstration.

Knutson, T. (2004). Thai cultural values: Smiles and sawasdee as implications for intercultural communication effectiveness. *Journal of Intercultural Communication Effectiveness 33*(3), 147–157.

Lawler, J. J. (1996). Diversity issues in South-East Asia: the case of Thailand. *International Journal of Manpower, 17*(4/5), 152–167.

Miller, J. B. (1976). *Toward a new psychology of women.* Boston: Beacon Press.

Minniti, M., Allen, I., & Langowitz, N. (2006). *Global entrepreneurship monitor: 2005 report on women and entrepreneurship.*

Minnitti, M., & Nardone, C. (in press). Being in someone else's shoes: The role of gender in nascent entrepreneurship. *Small Business Economics.*

Morris, M. H., Miyasuki, N. N., Watters, C. E., & Coombes, S. M. (2006). The dilemma of growth: Understanding venture size choices of women entrepreneurs. *Journal of Small Business Management, 44*(2), 221–244.

O'Gorman, C., & Terjesen, S. (2006). Financing the celtic tigress: Venture financing and informal investment in Ireland. *Venture Capital, 8*(1), 69–88.

Organization for Economic Cooperation and Development (OECD). (2000). *OECD small and medium enterprise outlook.* Paris: Author.

Siengthai, S., & Leelakulthanit, O. (1993–94). Women in management in Thailand: Parcipation for national prosperity. *International Studies of Management and Organization, 23*(4), 87–102.

Star Group. (2006). *Leading women entrepreneurs of the world conference, Bangkok, March.* Media Kit.

Strauss, A., & Corbin, J. (1990). *Basics of qualitative research: Grounded theory procedures and techniques.* Newbury Park, CA: Sage.

Szerb, L., Rappai, G., Makra, Z., & Terjesen, S. (in press). Informal investments in transition: Motivations, characteristics, and classifications in eastern Europe. *Small Business Economics.*

Tatler. (2006). *A woman's golden touch.*

United Nations Development Programme (UNDP). (2006). *Gender empowerment index.*

Virasa, T., Hunt, B., Shannon, R., & Min, T. Z. (2006). *Global entrepreneurship monitor: Thailand report.*

Viravan, C. (1998). *Thailand country report: Economic contribution of women in business in APEC Economies: Situation and recommendation.* The Federation of Business and Professional Women's Associations of Thailand under the Royal Patronage of Her Majesty the Queen. Bangkok.

CHAPTER 10

WOMEN ENTREPRENEURSHIP CONTEXT IN LATIN AMERICA

An Exploratory Study in Chile

José Ernesto Amorós and Olga Pizarro Stiepović

INTRODUCTION

There is no doubt that the progress made by women in entrepreneurship activities around the world represent an interesting factor to be taken into consideration when studying economic development and social progress (Minniti, Arenius, & Langowitz, 2005; Minniti, Allen, & Langowitz, 2006). At present, women represent more than one third of all people involved in entrepreneurship activities around the world. This phenomenon is not absent in Latin America where women have access to more important jobs through the generation of new companies. However, when the indicators of emerging countries are compared, and in this case the South American ones with a more advanced economy, it can be seen that women tend to get less involved in entrepreneurship activities. The gender gap in the labor field widens; this is one of the most important demographic phenomenon of the second half of the 20th century. This coincides with what was written by Heller (2004, p. 26): "[When management is studied]... one of the

The Perspective of Women's Entrepreneurship in the Age of Globalization, pages 109–126

109

basic principles pointed out is that 'the functions are neutral' when referring to management. This means that there is no indication in any administrative procedure manual that the functions of planning, management, control and supervision must be wielded by men." However, daily practice shows that only a few women are doing so; these administrative functions are generally and traditionally done by men.

Entrepreneurship activities by women are diverse and they cover almost all sectors of economic activities. Nevertheless, gender differences are still important, above all whenever we measure the motivation for getting started (Minniti & Nardone, in press). In proportion, it is men who are still in a majority when it comes to getting started, and they are more oriented toward searching for opportunities and, so, women are proportionally more in terms of getting started out of a necessity for doing so (Minniti, Allen, & Langowitz, 2006; Verheul, Uhlaner, & Thurik, 2003). Different authors point out that the different pattern in occupations between men and women is the result of a series of factors such as interests, socialization, institutional factors, and discrimination (e.g., Reskin & Hartman, 1985).

A report from the Women Center for Business Studies (*Centro de Estudios Empresariales de la Mujer*) (CEEM[1]) (2006a, p. 1) mentions that "The participation of women in economic activities is a growing phenomenon. In Chile, according to the 2002 census, 46.7% of all women between 25 and 54 years of age are working. There is a positive correlation between the rate of feminine participation in the labor market and a country per capita income. Although this ratio is not a cause in itself, it does show us that in more developed countries with per capita income levels threefold that of Chile, the rate of feminine participation is far higher than in Chile; around 80%." With respect to the business activity of women in Chile, the last General Homes and Population Survey (2006), made by the National Institute of Statistics (*Instituto Nacional de Estadísticas* [INE]), shows another interesting phenomenon: 33% of total employers in Chile are women. According to another survey made by INE during the first semester of 2004 related to small and medium enterprises, 13% of the owners of small- and mediumsized businesses are women. These indicators reflects the fact that it is useful to understand how women are involved in the creation of new companies and, therefore, consider that entrepreneurship led by them is also a key factor when it comes to increasing the dynamism of the economy (de Bruin, Brush, & Welter, 2006).

This work analyzes, in an exploratory approach, some women entrepreneurship dynamics indicators. We have analyzed these indicators from the data provided by the Global Entrepreneurship Monitor Report 2005 (GEM) as well as a series of interviews that provide us additional qualitative information. The rest of the work is structured in the following way: Section 2 deals with some relevant literature on women and entrepreneurship activities. In the third section is an analysis and a description of the variables related to the study; section 4 shows the results and, finally, section 5 features our conclusions.

LITERATURE REVIEW

Gender and Entrepreneurship Activities

Our way of approaching the issue of entrepreneurship begins from a perspective of the Gartner model (1985) suggested by Valencia (2005). This model features four dimensions from which entrepreneurship can be assessed. This is helpful for specifically analyzing female entrepreneurship. The dimensions are the individual (in our case, the characteristics of the entrepreneurs themselves); second, the organization (referring to the business model in which they are working or the one they feel more comfortable with); third, the prior process (what qualifications existed prior to beginning a business); and, finally, the environment (environmental factors).

With the individual dimension, the GEM Report on Women (Minniti et al., 2005; Minniti, Allen, & Langowitz, 2006) suggested that entrepreneurship in developed countries comes from women with a higher education as opposed to entrepreneurship in developing countries where less academic preparation is observed. In addition, Tiffin (2004) has shown that established businesspersons have, in a great majority of cases, higher education (p. 275). This argument is consistent with the fact that access to higher levels of education enables women to have the option to higher job positions and higher responsibility within the organizations hierarchy.

With the organization dimension, according to Rosa and Hamilton (1994), women entrepreneurship has not shown great differences, except with the issue of the number of associates. In the case of female entrepreneurship, it is usual that the number of partners to be less and they seek out family members as their first partners. For other authors like Watson (2002), the way in which businesses are developed do not have differences between men and women; while other authors sustain that the difference lies in women that feel that their possibilities diminish when competing with men (Sexton & Robinson, 1989). Gatewood, Shaver, and Gartner (1995) focus on getting started in business. Alsos and Ljunggren (1998) demonstrate a difference in the process of beginning a business, specifically with the business plan. This is strengthened in the case of the GEM, Women in Chile (Amorós & Pizarro, 2006) where the growth difference in business expectations can be seen, depending on the number of new contracts waiting to be entered into.

The environmental dimension is perceived, according to Fay and Williams (1993) and Coleman (1998), as women suffering from gender discrimination when they go in search of startup capital for their businesses, which is only offset by higher education and a good level of contacts. Greene, Brush, Hart, and Shapiro (1999) show that many women are excluded, for example, from venture capital mechanisms. The CEEM Report (2006a) indicates that the main barriers perceived by businesswomen are lack of capital (34.2%) and low autonomy of women (24.7%). In respect to financing, it is indicated that there are ways of financing micro and small businesses, but women do not have the necessary information to achieve it. Without this information, they encounter a problem commonly solved by including in the business a partner with capital.

Empirical Evidence: An Approach from GEM

The phenomenon of entrepreneurship is complex and related to various factors. It is for this reason that it is difficult trying to make one sole approach that explains entrepreneurship in a certain country. The GEM project has made an extensive approach (not by any means exhaustive), which furnishes a series of measures that enable us to get to know entrepreneurship and some of its implications in the country (Minniti, Bygrave, & Autio, 2006).

So as to get a better understanding of how women are related to the entrepreneurship cycle, the GEM distinguishes between entrepreneurs as being those who have not paid any salaries for over 3 months; new entrepreneurs: those who have paid salaries in the period between 3 and 42 months; and established businesswomen, those who have developed a company or a business and who have paid salaries for over 42 months. When both are taken into consideration, the new or nascent entrepreneurs, this indicator is called an entrepreneurship in its initial stages.[2] The first indicator that the GEM shows estimates of the proportion of participation of the adult economy active population[3] in the country that is directly involved in the initial entrepreneurship stages. Figure 10.1 shows these indicators and in the appendix are the results of the countries taking part in the GEM in 2005.

The GEM study framework explains the different motivations that women (and men) have when they are looking to start a new business or a company. This motivation may be the result of a desire to run a business opportunity or perhaps because labor conditions are unsatisfactory or women did not fund a stable job, which points to a necessity entrepreneurship. Figure 10.2 shows all the countries that took part in the GEM 2005 with the female entrepreneurship indicators depending on motivation.

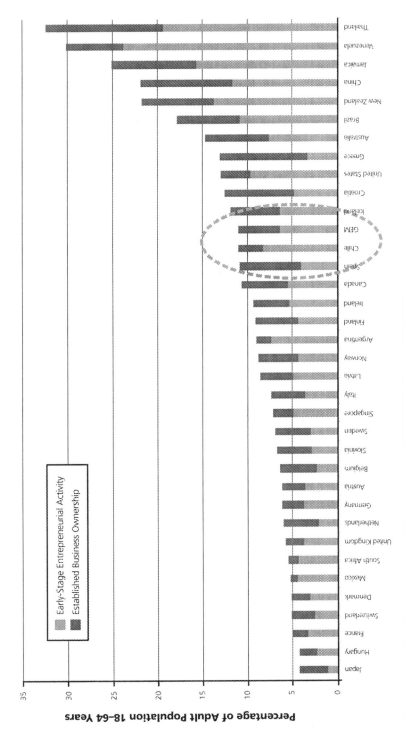

Figure 10.1. Female entrepreneurship per country, GEM 2005. *Source:* GEM 2005

113

114

Figure 10.2. Motivation for female entrepreneurship per country, GEM 2005. *Source:* GEM 2005

As can be observed, motivation as a result of opportunity predominates, but the ratio of opportunity to necessity varies importantly between countries (the graph is ordered according to this ratio from less to more). This is also true for men, but it is more revealing in female entrepreneurship. In proportion, it is men who, in a greater majority, are more oriented toward the search for opportunities (Amorós et al., 2006) and, as a result, it is women who are proportionally getting started out of necessity (Minniti, Allen, & Langowitz, 2006; Verheul et al., 2003). The same figure shows that the countries with the larger percentages of opportunities are those that have a higher level of development. Generally speaking, it is these countries that, given their conditions of stability and diversity in labor markets, show higher ratios of opportunity versus necessity.

DATA AND METHODOLOGY

Classification of Entrepreneurship Attitudes and Perceptions

As was explained, the GEM's methodology enables entrepreneurship initiatives can be catalogued into three categories: nascent entrepreneurs (under 3 months in the business), new entrepreneurs (3 to 42 months), and established ones (over 42 months). This classification is obtained from a survey of the adult population. For the 2005 period, in Chile this survey was applied over a sample of 2,000 persons among the adult population, of which 1,992 were valid (99%). The number of women who responded correctly to the survey was 1,326 (66.34%). Out of the total acceptable answers (men and women), a total of 1,278 (64%) had to answer the four questions relating to individual attitudes regarding entrepreneurship that can be related to the Gartner (1985) dimensions. The proportion of women who answered these questions was 64.1%. For each question, there were four possible answers: "yes," "no," "not known," or "refused."

The questions in relation to Gartner's dimensions, between parentheses, are as follows:

(a) Do you personally know anybody who has begun a new business or company in the last 2 years? (Organization and environment)
(b) Do you think that in the next 6 months there will be good opportunities for beginning a new business or company where you live? (Environment and prior process)
(c) Do you think you have the know-how, skills, and experience necessary to begin a new business or company? (Prior process)
(d) Does fear play a part in your not beginning a new business? (Individual)

The number of affirmative answers per gender and category of enterprises enables us to begin an exploratory analysis into comparing whether there are any significant differences between the groups, placing special emphasis on the gender variable. By types of variables, we resorted to a series of nonparametrical tests in order to analyze the different answers. We used a series of *Mann-Whitney U* tests to compare whether there really were any significant differences between men and women for each question. In addition, we used a series of *chi-squared* tests as an adjustment in order to compare affirmative answers per gender and type of enterprise. Finally, we compared independence between the four questions as a *Friedman* test.

Interviews with Experts

The GEM methodology includes making a series of in-depth interviews and a standardized survey of a group of no less than 30 experts on entrepreneurship issues. The aim of this survey was to have a measurement of factors or variables that influence enterprise in the country itself (Reynolds, Bosma, & Autio, 2005). Of the 82 questions this survey contains, there is a section with five questions that are directly related to gender and feminine opportunities to begin an enterprise. These questions were:

1. In my country, there are sufficient social services available that enable women to continue working, even after they have had children.

2. In my country, beginning a business or a company is a socially acceptable career move for a woman.

3. In my country, women are encouraged to become independent businesswomen or begin a new business.

4. In my country, men and women are equally exposed to good opportunities when it comes to beginning a new business or company.

5. In my country, men and women have the same level of know-how and skills to be able to begin a new business or company.

Analyzing these questions enables us to gain additional elements in order to get to know the general situation regarding female entrepreneurship and also to establish some sort of relationship between the indicators in the survey to the adult population and the experts' opinion, emphasizing how the environment of the dynamics of entrepreneurship is perceived. During 2005, we gathered the opinions and surveyed 33 experts. In addition, in order to increase feminine representativeness in it, we consulted a panel of 16 businesswomen, using these same questions during the first few months of 2006.

In order to measure the perception of each question, the Likert scale consisting of five points[4] was used, which enabled us to form an opinion on each one of the variables. A range of answers was analyzed in order to identify in which direction the majority of them were heading. For that, we graphed the percentages of persons who disagreed (completely + partially) against the percentage that was in agreement (completely + partially). Besides, the answers that showed no preference were ruled out (meaning the replies were "neither here nor there"), recalculating the percentages over those that did have a marked preference. This methodology has the advantage that it ruled out any variances in the answers.

RESULTS

Perception of the Adult Population

In a first analysis, we ruled out the answers "not known and 'not answered," because their rate of answer is not critical and happens to be less than 0.3%. The four *Friedman* tests, one for each type of enterprise, comparing the questions, were significant at a level of 0.05, so we can conclude that at least the answers to each one of the four questions differ from each other and there might not be any "effect" of answering "yes" systematically to each one.

Table 10.1 shows the proportion of affirmative answers per gender, expressed in the rows, and per type of enterprise, represented in the columns for each one of the four questions. Likewise, the significances of the *Mann-Whitney U* and the *Chi-squared* are shown for each type of activity.

The results of the nonparametric tests on each one of the questions show that for the three types of enterprises, there are no significant differences between men and women as regards the four factors of perception. The lower rate of the *Mann-Whitney U* test refers to the fear of failure factor when it comes to beginning a new business with nascent entrepreneurs. Albeit not significant, it gives us some idea that probably women are more afraid of beginning a business in its early stages, but what is important is that, like men, they are prepared to do so.

Regarding the persons who said they did not have an enterprise, the results show us that there are indeed significant differences both in men and women, as well as in the percentages of affirmative answers. This leads us to have a first approach inasmuch that women who are not involved in any enterprise perceive differently the factors that are inherent in the dynamics of entrepreneurship, and as a possible consequence, this shows signs that the women interviewed did have "greater disadvantages" when it came to beginning an enterprise.

TABLE 10.1
Factors That Influence the Perception of Entrepreneurs per Gender and Stage of the Enterprise (Percentage of affirmative answers and significance tests)

	No enterprise	Nascent entrepreneurs	New entrepreneurs	Enterprise already established
Do you personally know anybody who has begun a new business or company in the last 2 years?				
Men	47.5%	71.7%	83.3%	74.2%
Women	35.5%	65.5%	66.7%	56.8%
Sig.	.000*	.470	.084	.137
(U. de Mann-Whitney)				
Sig(c^2)	.000*	.467	.083	.134
Do you think that in the next 6 months there will be good opportunities for beginning a new business or company where you live?				
Men	46.7%	60.9%	73.8%	74.2%
Women	36.0%	60.3%	66.7%	54.1%
Sig.	.003*	.850	.931	.175
(U de Mann-Whitney)				
Sig(c^2)	.003*	.850	.931	.171
Do you think you have the know-how, skills, and experience necessary to begin a new business or company?				
Men	66.1%	91.3%	85.7%	96.8%
Women	55.9%	81.9%	89.7%	86.5%
Sig.	.001*	.149	.584	.224
(U de Mann-Whitney)				
Sig(c^2)	.001*	.147	.582	.221
Does fear play a part in your not beginning a new business?				
Men	31.6%	26.1%	19.0%	22.6%
Women	44.4%	43.1%	15.4%	24.5%
Sig.	.000*	.063	.629	.718
(U de Mann-Whitney)				
Sig(c^2)	.000*	.062	.627	.716

* 0.05 significance.

Analyzing the Interviews with Experts

As mentioned in the methodology section, a part of the GEM study gathers opinions from 33 national experts on such topics as gender and entrepreneurship. Figure 10.3 shows the results of the specific gender questions. The answers that were obtained from 16 women entrepreneurs are shown in Figure 10.4. Although there are some differences between both groups, we did not find they were statistically significant.[5] Figure 10.5 shows the results of all of the interviews.

In the case of the experts' opinions, these show a clear view of gender inequality regarding entrepreneurship. On the one hand, it is suggested that one-third of those surveyed see differences at a level of know-how and skills when it comes to beginning a business. It is also explained that, in the opinion of the experts, women are not encouraged to begin businesses even when it is a socially acceptable move and that the existence of the support of some social services is considered.

In the case of female entrepreneurs, even when there are differences from their perspective as regards the level of know-how and skills to begin a business or a company, they perceive fewer differences than the panel of experts. One of the aspects that did not show any significant differences was the perception that men and women are equally exposed to good opportunities when it comes to beginning a business or a company and, in this case, both groups coincide that there are marked differences. Female entrepreneurs view less favorably that beginning a business is socially acceptable for a woman. Lastly, the entrepreneurs consider that social services are available for a woman to continue working, considerably better than the opposite opinion of the group of experts.

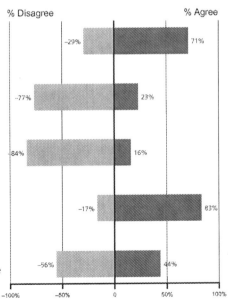

Figure 10.3. Experts' opinions on entrepreneurship and gender issues ($n = 33$).
Source: GEM Women and Entrepreneurship in Chile 2005/2006

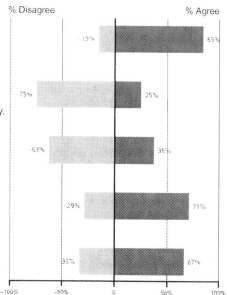

Figure 10.4.   The opinion of women business owners on entrepreneurship and gender issues (*n* = 16). *Source:* GEM Women and Entrepreneurship in Chile 2005/2006

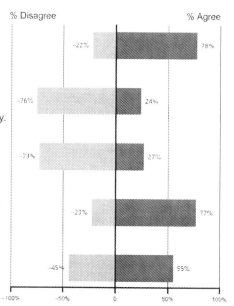

Figure 10.5.   The opinion of the interviewees on entrepreneurship and gender issues (*n* = 49). *Source:* GEM Women and Entrepreneurship in Chile 2005/2006

When comparing both graphs, we find that, culturally, the perception exists that opportunities and incentives are unfavorable when it comes to women beginning businesses. Even though there is a favorable view regarding preparation in both groups' know-how and skills and a socially favorable perception that women can indeed become entrepreneurs.

So, the conclusion can be reached that even when it is socially acceptable for women to begin new businesses, they are further away from the opportunities and there are not sufficient incentives in our country to do so.

The latest study conducted by the CEEM (2006b) reflects that 61% of entrepreneurs had worked as employees previously and that opportunity is the most representative of reasons to begin a new business. So, the question "In my country, men and women are equally exposed to good opportunities to begin a business or a company" becomes fundamental in the case of women. Should this perception and difference in gender persist, a generation of new companies will find itself affected.

CONCLUSIONS

There is no doubt that the progress made by women in terms of quality and quantity in entrepreneurship represents an interesting factor to be taken into account within spheres of economic development and social progress in Latin America. Evidently, Chile is not the exception and we look kindly on how women assume an ever more important role in the generation of new companies. Nevertheless, there is still a long way to go, above all if we compare Chile's indicators with some of those from more advanced nations.

In Chile, female entrepreneurship is diverse and it covers almost all sectors of the economy. However, gender differences are still important, especially when we measure the available incentives for getting started. Generally, in Latin America exists a clear vision of gender inequity with respect to entrepreneurship. In Chile, there exists a cultural perception that opportunities and incentives are unfavorable for women to begin businesses, even when they have the abilities, knowledge, and a socially favorable perception when they begin to entrepreneur. In proportion, men starting a new venture are more oriented toward searching opportunities, so it is women who get started more out of necessity. In addition, we find that women get started in sectors of the economy more oriented toward consumers (sales) and, although many are genuine opportunities, in many cases they are not activities with a great benefit. One indicator from the GEM study of Women in Chile (Amorós & Pizarro, 2006) shows that only 13% of women entrepreneurs believe that their company or business will have a high impact or growth in 5 years' time.

Other results from the report show that women entrepreneurs in Chile are older when compared to other countries within the scope of the GEM. Also, female entrepreneurs say they are stably employed, either on their own initiative or because they have a parallel job. In their majority, they have received a higher education and they are married or at least living with someone. On reflection, although this is not a categorical fact, women entrepreneurship might be related to stability in the family but, unfortunately, in this country, just as the conclusions drawn from the interviews with experts and female entrepreneurship show, it is perceived that women are not encouraged to become independent entrepreneurs or begin a new business. It is generally thought that a company managed by a women is a supplementary activity (i.e., an "extension of the family"). However, it is very encouraging to see that women, in addition to the traditional family role society has endowed them with, are developing entrepreneurial activities with a great capacity for it. For this reason, it is very important to view the phenomenon of female entrepreneurship as a positive sign of social development and progress.

Finally, emphasizing the role that women in our society play is becoming more and more relevant and far-reaching, and it brings to light particularities that have to be tackled as such. As indicated by the Code of Good Labor Practices,[6] about no discrimination for the central administration of the Government of Chile, social, family, and work relations have experienced strong changes. These are mainly owed to a growing incorporation and participation of women in the workforce, and the consequent changes in family organizations. Without this meaning a definite fact, women entrepreneurship could be related with the stability of the family.

This work, even though exploratory, will help to understand and stress the role of women entrepreneurs in Latin America. Some results are useful both for gender entrepreneurship studies, as well as being an important point of reflection for public, educational, and social institutions, which are able to wield influence through policies, programs, or initiatives that encourage and buttress women's entrepreneurship activities. Future research will be able to provide us with a better perspective and furnish more and better data for reaching conclusions and inferences on the complex phenomenon of entrepreneurship. In the meantime, we believe that efforts such as this work, within the parameters and strictures of the GEM, are of great help when it comes to viewing better women within the context of entrepreneurship and, better still, within the context of the country's economic and social development.

Other topics being able to analyze in greater depth are as venture capital for women who want to start a business (Orser, Riding, & Manley, 2006) and suggest public policies relating to financing. For developing countries, it is necessary to have not only new enterprises, but also be of greater impact on everything related to hiring people. As companies grow and hiring increases, the likelihood that companies will live on over time will encourage other companies to appear and be of benefit to the country.

NOTES

1. The CEEM is a joint venture between the Faculty of Economy and Business of Universidad del Desarrollo, and the Women Business Organization *Mujeres Empresarias*. For more information, see www.mujeresempresarias.cl

2. In previous editions of the GEM, this measure of entrepreneurship is called the TEA index (Total Entrepreneurial Activity).

3. The standardized source of the structure of the total population of countries taking part was the US Census Bureau International Database (http://www.census.gov/ipc/www/didbnew.html. The age range from 18 to 64 years of age is the one taken in all of the samples from all of the countries and is considered as the range into which the large majority of a country's labor force fits.

4. Completely disagreed, partially disagreed, neither agreed or disagreed, partially agreed, and completely agreed.

5. The Kolmogorov-Smirnov Z Test with two independent samples $p > 0.05$.

6. Chilean Government Document, December 2006.

APPENDIX
Entrepreneurship in Different GEM Countries per Gender, 2005

Country	Entrepreneurship during initial stages		Established entrepreneurs		Total entrepreneurship	
	Men	Women	Men	Women	Men	Women
Germany	6.92%	3.82%	5.99%	2.35%	12.91%	6.17%
Argentina	11.62%	7.39%	8.38%	1.58%	20.00%	8.97%
Australia	14.17%	7.55%	12.08%	7.09%	26.25%	14.64%
Austria	6.90%	3.66%	5.10%	2.58%	12.00%	6.24%
Belgium	5.43%	2.42%	7.23%	4.03%	12.66%	6.45%
Brazil	**11.82%**	**10.83%**	**13.33%**	**7.00%**	**25.15%**	**17.83%**
Canada	13.11%	5.56%	9.72%	5.09%	22.83%	10.65%
Chile	**14.15%**	**8.21%**	**4.82%**	**2.76%**	**18.97%**	**10.97%**
China	15.73%	11.60%	16.06%	10.27%	31.79%	21.87%
Croatia	9.78%	2.58%	4.74%	2.61%	14.52%	5.19%
Denmark	6.40%	3.09%	6.56%	2.12%	12.96%	5.21%
Slovenia	5.79%	2.92%	8.74%	3.78%	14.53%	6.70%
Spain	7.17%	4.15%	8.75%	6.68%	15.92%	10.83%
USA	15.24%	9.65%	6.01%	3.35%	21.25%	13.00%
Finland	5.52%	4.41%	12.43%	4.73%	17.95%	9.14%
France	7.40%	3.33%	2.76%	1.79%	10.16%	5.12%
Greece	9.68%	3.37%	11.36%	9.63%	21.04%	13.00%
Netherlands	6.58%	2.11%	7.35%	3.94%	13.93%	6.05%
Hungary	1.39%	2.39%	2.08%	1.95%	3.47%	4.34%
Ireland	14.21%	5.48%	12.26%	3.88%	26.47%	9.36%
Iceland	14.82%	6.40%	9.05%	5.48%	23.87%	11.88%
Italy	6.17%	3.70%	9.17%	3.64%	15.34%	7.34%
Jamaica	**18.37%**	**15.69%**	**9.57%**	**9.49%**	**27.94%**	**25.18%**
Japan	3.20%	1.20%	7.67%	3.11%	10.87%	4.31%
Latvia	8.47%	5.02%	6.57%	3.60%	15.04%	8.62%
Mexico	**7.38%**	**4.55%**	**3.11%**	**0.77%**	**10.49%**	**5.32%**
Norway	13.91%	4.47%	10.10%	4.38%	24.01%	8.85%
New Zealand	21.65%	13.75%	13.83%	8.03%	35.48%	21.78%
UK	8.67%	3.74%	8.06%	2.08%	16.73%	5.82%
Singapore	9.56%	5.04%	7.49%	2.15%	17.05%	7.19%
South Africa	5.88%	4.49%	1.63%	1.00%	7.51%	5.49%
Sweden	5.08%	2.99%	8.68%	3.91%	13.76%	6.90%
Switzerland	7.28%	4.89%	11.86%	7.59%	19.14%	12.48%
Thailand	22.20%	19.33%	15.09%	13.15%	37.29%	32.48%
Venezuela	**26.13%**	**23.86%**	**10.93%**	**6.25%**	**37.06%**	**30.11%**
GEM	**10.51%**	**6.39%**	**8.53%**	**4.62%**	**19.04%**	**11.01%**

REFERENCES

Alsos, G., & E. Ljunggren. (1998). Does the business start-up process differ by gender? A longitudinal study of nascent entrepreneurs. *Frontiers of Entrepreneurship,* Babson College.

Acs Z. J., Arenius, P. Hay, M., & Minniti, M. (2005). *Global Entrepreneurship Monitor, Executive Report 2004.* Babson College and the London Business School, Babson Park, MA.

Amorós, J. E., Cortés, P., Echecopar, G., & Flores, T. (2006). *Global Entrepreneurship Monitor, National Report, Chile 2005.* Universidad de Adolfo Ibáñez and the Universidad del Desarrollo, Santiago, Chile.

Amorós, J. E., & Pizarro, O. (2006). *Global Entrepreneurship Monitor, Report on Women and Entrepreneurship, Chile,* 2005/2006. Universidad del Desarrollo, Santiago, Chile.

Coleman, S. (1998). Access to capital: A comparison of men and women-owned small businesses. *Frontiers of Entrepreneurship,* Babson College.

CEEM. (2006a). *Characteristics and profile of Chilean women in the business world: executives and businesspersons.* Report 1. Universidad Del Desarrollo, Santiago, Chile.

CEEM. (2006b). *Comparative study of the quality of life: men and women in the labor market.* Report 2. Universidad de Desarrollo, Santiago, Chile.

De Bruin, A., Brush, C., & Welter, F. (2006). Introduction to the Special Issue: Towards Building Cumulative Knowledge on Women's Entrepreneurship. *Entrepreneurship Theory and Practice, 30*(5), 585–593.

Fay, M., & Williams, L. (1993). Gender bias and the availability of business loans. *Journal of Business Venturing, 8*(4), 363–376.

Gartner, W. (1985). A conceptual framework for describing the phenomenon of new venture creation. *Academy of Management Review, 10*(4), 696–706.

Gatewood, E. J., Shaver, K. G., & Gartner, W. B. (1995). A longitudinal study on cognitive factors influencing start-up behaviors and success at venture creation. *Journal of Business Venturing, 10*(5), 371–391.

Greene, P., Brush, C., Hart, M., & Shapiro, P. (1999). Exploration of the venture capital industry: is gender an issue? *Frontiers of Entrepreneurship,* Babson College.

Heller, L. (2004). *New voices in leadership: Dilemmas and strategies of working women.* Buenos Aires: Latinoamericano Publications Group.

Kanter, R. (1994). Foreword. In N. Nichols (Ed.), *Reach for the top: Women and the changing facts of work life* (114–125). Cambridge, MA: Harvard Business School Press.

Minniti, M., Allen, I. E., & Langowitz, N. (2006) *Global Entrepreneurship Monitor, 2005. Report on Women and Entrepreneurship.* Babson College and the London Business School, Babson Park, MA.

Minniti, M., Arenius, P., & Langowitz, N. (2005). *Global Entrepreneurship Monitor, 2004. Report on Women and Entrepreneurship.* Babson College and the London Business School, Babson Park, MA.

Minniti, M., Bygrave, W. D., & Autio, E. (2006) *Global Entrepreneurship Monitor, Executive Report 2005.* Babson College and the London Business School, Babson Park, MA.

Minniti, M., & Nardone, C. (in press). Being in someone else's shoes: Gender and nascent entrepreneurship. *Small Business Economics Journal.*

Orser, B. J., Riding, A. L., & Manley, K. (2006). Women entrepreneurs and financial capital. *Entrepreneurship Theory and Practice, 30*(5), 643–665.

Reskin, B., & Hartman, H. (1985): *Women's work, men's work: Sex segregation on the job.* Washington, DC: National Academy Press.

Reynolds, P., Bosma, N., & Autio, E. (2005). Global Entrepreneurship Monitor: Data collection design and implementation 1998–2003. *Small Business Economics, 24*(3), 205–231.

Rosa, P., & Hamilton, D. (1994). Gender and ownership in U.K. of small firms. *Entrepreneurship Theory and Practice, 18*(3), 11–27.

Sexton, E. A., & Robinson, P. B. (1989). The economic and demographic determinants of self-employment. *Frontiers of Entrepreneurship*, Babson College.

Tiffin, S. (2004). *Entrepreneurship in Latin America: Perspectives on education and innovation.* Westport, CT: Praeger.

Valencia, M. (2005, December). *The female-entrepreneurship field: 1990–2004.* Paper presented during the fourth annual meeting of the Spanish-American Academy of Management, Lisbon.

Verheul, I., Uhlaner, L., & Thurik, R. (2003). *Business accomplishments, gender and entrepreneurial self-image.* SACELES-paper N200312. The Netherlands.

Watson, J. (2002). Comparing the performance of male and female controlled businesses: Relating output to input. *Entrepreneurship Theory and Practice, 26*(3), 91–100.

PART III

SUITABLE FINANCIAL ARRANGEMENTS THAT SUPPORT FEMALE ENTREPRENEURSHIP

CHAPTER 11

DO WOMEN BENEFIT FROM MICROCREDIT

Aneel Karnani

INTRODUCTION

The Nobel Peace Price for 2006 was awarded to the Grameen Bank in Bangladesh and its founder, Muhammad Yunus, is a pioneer of the microcredit movement. The Nobel Committee affirmed that microcredit must play a "major part" in eliminating poverty. The central objective of the Grameen Bank has been to "reverse the age-old vicious circle of 'low income, low savings, and low investment', into a virtuous circle of 'low income, injection of credit, investment, more income, more savings, more investment, more income.'" The United Nations, having designated 2005 as the international year of microcredit, declares on its website, "currently microentrepreneurs use loans as small as $100 to grow thriving businesses and, in turn, provide their families, leading to strong and flourishing local economies." Commercial banks, such as ICICI in India, are expanding into microcredit.

Microcredit organizations have primarily targeted women as their clients. Yunus is reported to have said "women have plans for themselves, for their children, about their home, the meals. They have a vision. A man wants to enjoy himself." Given this intensity of interest and the resources devoted to it, it is reasonable to ask how much do poor women really benefit from microcredit.

The Perspective of Women's Entrepreneurship in the Age of Globalization, pages 129–136
Copyright © 2007 by Information Age Publishing

EMPOWERMENT

Microcredit often yields noneconomic benefits such as increasing self-esteem and social cohesion, and empowering women (Sabharwal, 2000). Microcredit enables women to contribute toward the household economy, leading to economic empowerment and increasing their intrahousehold bargaining power. Microcredit also facilitates women to move from positions of marginalization within the household decision-making process and exclusion within the community, to greater centrality, inclusion, and voice. The social processes of microcredit lead to strengthening the personal and social dimensions of women's empowerment. This results in increased self-esteem and self-worth for women and a greater sense of awareness of social and political issues, leading to increased mobility and reduced seclusion of women.

But there is some empirical evidence suggesting that microcredit does not always result in increased empowerment for women. Credit by itself cannot overcome patriarchal systems of control at household and community levels. Women's control over financial resources is probably a key factor in explaining these mixed results. It seems that a significant fraction of women, in spite of having *access* to credit, do not have *control* over the loans contracted or the income generated from the microenterprises (Sebstad & Chen, 1996).

ECONOMIC IMPACT

Overall, microcredit does yield noneconomic benefits of empowering women. It also helps the poor smooth consumption over periods of cyclical or unexpected crisis, and thus reduces vulnerability (Morduch, 1998). But, that is not enough; the key issue is whether microcredit helps eradicate poverty. *The Economist* magazine concluded that while "heart-warming case studies abound, rigorous empirical analyses are rare" ("Macro Credit," 2006). A few studies have even found that microcredit has a negative impact on poverty; poor households simply become poorer through the additional burden of debt (Hulme & Mosley, 1996). However, most studies suggest that microcredit is beneficial, but only to a limited extent. The reality is less attractive than the promise (Dichter, 2006).

Why is microcredit not more effective? The problem lies not with microcredit but rather with microenterprises. The United Nations' declaration that microentrepreneurs use loans to grow thriving businesses leading to flourishing economies is hype. A client of microcredit is an entrepreneur in the literal sense: she raises the capital, manages the business, and is the residual claimant of the earnings. But, the current usage of the word "entrepreneur" requires more than the literal definition. Entrepreneurship is the engine of Joseph Schumpeter's dynamism of "creative destruction." An entrepreneur is a person of vision and creativity who converts a new idea into a successful innovation, into a new business model. Some clients of microcredit are certainly true entrepreneurs, and have created thriving businesses—these are the heart-warming anecdotes. But the vast majority of microcredit clients are caught in subsistence activities with no prospect of competitive advantage. The self-employed poor usually have no specialized skills and often practice multiple occupations (Banerjee & Duflo, 2006). Many of these businesses operate at too small a scale. The median business operated by the poor has no paid staff; most of these businesses have very few assets as well. With low skills, little capital, and no scale economies, these businesses operate in arenas with low entry barriers and too much competition; they have low productivity and lead to meager earnings that cannot lift their owners out of poverty.

This should not be too surprising. Most people do not have the skills, vision, creativity, and persistence to be true entrepreneurs. Even in developed countries with high levels of education and infrastructure, about 90% of the labor force are employees rather than entrepreneurs. Even with greater availability of financial services in developed countries, only a small fraction has used credit for entrepreneurial purposes. Most clients of microcredit are not microentrepreneurs by choice and would gladly take a factory job at reasonable wages if possible. We should not romanticize the idea of the "poor as entrepreneurs." The International Labor Organization (ILO) uses a more appropriate term, "own account workers."

EMPLOYMENT

Creating opportunities for steady employment at reasonable wages is the best way to take people out of poverty. The ILO states that "nothing is more fundamental to poverty reduction than employment." In development economics there is much theoretical and empirical support for the increasing preponderance of wage labor in a developing economy. It is instructive to look at the pattern of poverty and employment over time in China, India, and Africa (which together account for about three-quarters of the poor in the world), using World Bank and ILO data (Majid, 2005).

	People below $2/day	
	Late 1980s	Late 1990s
China	67.4%	50.1%
India	83.2%	78.8%
Africa	76.1%	76.1%

	Employment/Population	
	Late 1980s	**Late 1990s**
China	51.0%	58.7%
India	29.5%	35.8%
Africa	33.4%	30.1%

In China, where the incidence of poverty has declined significantly, a large and growing fraction of the population is employed. In Africa, where the incidence of poverty has remained unchanged, a small and shrinking fraction of the population is employed. India's performance lies somewhere in between. India's efforts at poverty reduction have been hampered by its poor performance in job creation. India's jobless growth is the result of a distorted emphasis on a capital-intensive and skill-intensive development path (Kochhar et al., 2006). Capital-intensive sectors, such as heavy manufacturing, and skill-intensive sectors, such as information technology, will not solve India's poverty problem. The trickle-down effects of general economic growth are too little and too slow. India needs to emphasize growth in labor-intensive, low-skill sectors such as light manufacturing, the garment industry, and tourism. Seven world-class Indian Institutes of Technology do not compensate for the 39% illiteracy rate.

SCALE ECONOMIES

Many people who have jobs are still stuck below the poverty line—the working poor. Whether an employee is "poor" or not depends on her wages, size of the household, and the income of other household members. It is not enough to create jobs; we also have to increase productivity such that the wages are high enough to enable the employees to rise above poverty.

	Working poor/Employment	
	Late 1980s	**Late 1990s**
China	79.6%	35.2%
India	75.0%	62.0%
Africa	63.4%	65.4%

On this dimension too, India's performance is mediocre and the situation in Africa is dismal. One cause of this poor growth in productivity in India is inadequate scale economies in its enterprises. The average firm size in India is less then one-tenth the comparable size in other emerging economies (Kochhar et al., 2006). The emphasis on microcredit will only make this problem worse.

Rather than lending $200–500 to women so that each can buy a swwing machine and set up a microenterprise manufacturing garments, it is much better to lend $100,000 to an entrepreneur with managerial capabilities and business acumen and help her to set up a garment manufacturing business employing 500 people. Now the business can exploit economies of scale, deploy specialized assets, and use modern business processes to generate value for both its owners and employees.

FAILURE OF PUBLIC SERVICES

Poverty cannot be defined only in economic terms; it is about a much broader set of needs that permit well-being. Amartya Sen, a Nobel Prize–winning economist, eloquently argues that development can be seen as a "process of expanding the real freedoms that people enjoy" (Sen, 2000). Social, cultural, and political freedoms are desirable in and of themselves, and also enablers of individual income growth. Services such as public safety, basic education, public health, and infrastructure nurture these freedoms, and increase the productivity and employability of the poor, and thus their income and well-being.

In recent years, the political ideology of the world has shifted decisively toward an increased role for markets and a correspondingly decreased role for the state. But the role of the state has certainly not been eliminated, nor should it be. The state is responsible for basic education, public health, water, sanitation, public safety, and infrastructure. The government in every developing country certainly professes to accept responsibility for these traditional functions. Yet, it has failed dismally to deliver on its promises.

As an example of the failure of public services, consider the case of India. The Indian economy is growing rapidly, the stock market is at an all-time high, Indian companies are expanding abroad, and a large middle class is emerging. It is the best of times. Contrast this with another India. There is persistent income inequality and gender inequality. Eighty percent of Indians are below the commonly used $2/day poverty line. Thirty-nine percent of adults are illiterate. Ten percent of boys and 25% of girls do not attend even primary school. Forty-nine percent of children are underweight for their age. Nine percent of children die in the first 5 years of their lives. Thirty-one percent of rural households and 9% of urban households do not have access to safe drinking water. Eighty-one percent of rural households and 19% of urban households do not have a toilet. Four hundred thousand children die of diarrhea (a waterborne disease) every year. The boom in the private sector has been accompanied by a significant failure of the state. The cost of this failure is borne disproportion-ably by the poor.

The rich often purchase these services from private enterprises. The middle class are the main beneficiaries of the public service expenditures. The poor have no or little access to these services, get very low-quality pub-lic services, or pay very high prices for private services. For example, the rich go to world-class private hospitals and clinics. The middle class has access to reasonable public health facilities. While public health centers do exist to serve rural and poor areas, these centers are grossly underfunded and understaffed. Even worse, the staff are underqualified, and are often absent. Children of the rich go to exclusive private schools. The middle class uses a mix of private and public schools. Children of the poor often do not go to school or go to low-quality public schools. In one survey, a quarter of the teachers were absent and another quarter were present but not teaching. Absentee rates for teachers and health workers are higher in poorer regions. The rich have ample access to clean water: they purchase bottled drinking water, drill private tube wells, and use booster pumps. The middle class settles for piped water even if only for a few hours a day. The poor have no or little access to a clean public water supply. The rich hire private guards. The middle class live in reasonably well-policed neighbor-hoods. The poor have little protection from thugs and criminals.

The burden of failure of public services is borne disproportionably by women, which exacerbates gender inequality. Lack of access to toilets poses a bigger problem for women because of anatomy, modesty, and susceptibil-ity to attack. Women often lose much time to hauling buckets of water over long distances. Women are more likely than men to need medical care; they are expected to care for sick family members, especially children. Girls attend school less often, especially in poor families.

MARKETS ARE NOT THE SOLUTION

There is a growing "neoliberal" movement that looks to the private sector for the solution to the failure of public services. There is much debate about whether the direct production of these services should be privatized. But, few would argue that the state can totally avoid its responsibilities. For example, if the water supply is privatized, the government needs to regu-late the rates or ensure that the poor have enough purchasing power to buy water. In the case of a "public good" such as sanitation and public health, the market cannot solve the problem. Even the late Milton Fried-man advocated the school voucher system, and not for the state to with-draw totally from the field of education. The state must be responsible for services when there is a natural monopoly (piped water), when it is a public good (public health), and for the sake of equity (education). When the state fails, the market might be a partial complement, but it cannot be a total substitute.

Business guru C.K. Prahalad has said, "If people have no sewage and drinking water, should we also deny them televisions and cell phones?" ("Selling to the Poor," 2005). Writing about the slums of Mumbai, he argues that the poor accept that access to running water is not a "realistic option" and therefore spend their income on things that they can get now that improve the quality of their lives (Prahalad & Hammond, 2002). This opens up a market, and he urges private companies to make significant profits by selling to the "bottom of the pyramid" (BOP).

The real issue that the BOP proposition glosses over is, why do the poor accept that access to running water is not a realistic option? Even if they do, why should we all accept this bleak view? Instead, we should emphasize the failure of government and attempt to correct it. Giving a "voice" to the poor is a central aspect of the development process. That is what the civil society, for example Oxfam (2006), is attempting to do. In many developing countries, an autocratic government has denied a voice to the poor. Even in developing countries with a representative democracy, the political process has been hijacked by various vested interests. The business community, bureaucrats, politicians, and the media are full of self-congratulations on the booming private sector—for example, on the increased penetration of cell phones. However, the representative image of a developing country is not a cell phone, but rather defecating in public. For example, of Mumbai's 18 million inhabitants, 50% defecate outside. There is no magic solution, but the starting point is passion and anger at the failure of the state to provide these basic services.

Appealing to private companies to help the poor on the grounds of corporate social responsibility has not been an effective strategy. But, we can demand that private companies at a minimum not drown out the voice of the poor. For example, sustaining a social movement to empower women is more difficult in the pervasive presence of sexist advertisements, such as those for Fair & Lovely, the whitening cream marketed by Unilever. Self-regulation by the private sector might be the solution.

The civil society, with good intentions, often tries to supply the services the state has failed to provide. The problem is that the civil society has neither the resources nor the economies of scale to provide these services to any significant degree. Instead, the civil society should attempt to strengthen the state, support the voice of the poor, and be a catalyst in the political process.

CONCLUSION

Microcredit has received much attention and has grown rapidly in recent years. Women, who account for the bulk of the clients of microcredit, have benefited in terms of increased self-esteem and empowerment. But, microcredit has not had a significant impact on alleviating poverty. The women run businesses with low skills, little capital, and no scale economies, and as a result do not earn enough to rise out of poverty. Creating employment and increasing productivity is the best solution to poverty. We should emphasize the role of the government in providing basic public services, which have a direct and significant impact on productivity.

REFERENCES

Banerjee, A., & Duflo, E. (2006). The economic lives of the poor. *Journal of Economic Perspectives, 21*(1), 141–167.

Dichter, T. W. (2006). *Hype and hope: The worrisome state of the microcredit movement.* Available at http://www.microfinancegateway.org/content/article/detail/31747

Hulme, D., & Mosley, P. (1996). *Finance against poverty.* New York: Routledge.

Kochhar, K., et al. (2006). India's pattern of development: What happened, what follows? *Journal of Monetary Economics, 53*(5), 1021–1026.

Macro credit. (2006, October 21). *The Economist.*

Majid, N. (2005). *On the evolution of employment structure in developing countries.* Employment Strategy Papers, International Labor Organization.

Morduch, J. (1998). *Does microfinance really help the poor?: New evidence from flagship programs in Bangladesh.* Harvard Institute of International Development and Hoover Institution, Stanford University. Available at http://www.wws.princeton.edu/~rpds/downloads/morduch_microfinance_poor.pdf

Oxfam. (2006). *In the public interest.* Oxfam International.

Prahalad, C. K., & Hammond, A. (2002). Serving the world's poor profitably. *Harvard Business Review, 80*(9).

Sabharwal, G. (2000). *From the margin to the mainstream. Micro-Finance Programmes and Women's Empowerment: The Bangladesh Experience.* Swansea: University of Wales. Available at http://www.gdrc.org/icm/wind/geeta.pdf

Sebstad, J., & Chen, G. (1996). *Overview of studies on the impact of microenterprise credit.* Washington, DC: AIMS, USAID.

Selling to the poor. (2005, April 17). *Time.*

Sen, A. (2000). *Development as freedom.* New York: Anchor Books.

CHAPTER 12

DIVERSITY PAYS FINANCIALLY

Murad Ali

INTRODUCTION

Diversity is an issue that has struck many managers and executives as a "feel good" program without much merit. There is increasing merit in a globalized economy that encourages diversity in the workforce. It is more than the right thing to do but is also based on sound business practices. Businesses that respect diversity find that they can reduce costs and increase profits that are not obtainable in monocultural workplaces.

Diversity has many benefits that include supporting fair and equitable treatment among men, allowing people to earn according to their own capacity, and encouraging the advancement of society and business. By allowing people to progress through societal ranks based on their own skill and worth and not on their race or religion, they are encouraging people to succeed. This constant striving of individuals to succeed creates a society that achieves more than one based on family size or cronyism.

Take the tribal country of Somalia and their continual failure to establish a working government as an example. The country has been plagued by cronyism and tribal politics for decades. The leading tribe who takes over control of the government refuses to allow competing tribes to take

The Perspective of Women's Entrepreneurship in the Age of Globalization, pages 137–145
Copyright © 2007 by Information Age Publishing
All rights of reproduction in any form reserved.

positions in the government. This philosophy does well in keeping the leading tribe in power but weakens the legitimacy of the government overall because other tribes are not invested in the idea.

The problems are further exacerbated because the most qualified individuals do not get the opportunity to help the government succeed because the leaders refuse to hire them. In so doing the government becomes full of people who are not qualified for their positions and are likely to be corrupt. In the end the administration is likely to not be effective, not utilize funding well, and not advance as a nation.

The nature of discrimination is inbred in our desire to survive as a race, as a family, and as a nation. When a Christian and Caucasian manager is interviewing a Muslim and dark-skinned foreigner there is little likelihood that either of them will feel comfortable around the other. This uncomfortable feeling is driven from our most basic instincts of survival. It wasn't long ago that one's tribe/village survived by promoting one's own kind. The more difference between the interviewee and the interviewer, the less likely an employment offer is to follow.

Thus discrimination is based in our very subconscious understanding of survival. Yet this doesn't mean that we can't avoid discrimination if we become aware of these urges. By understanding the nature of our discrimination we can apply our analytical and logical minds to hire the best candidate out of the bunch. Awareness is 50% of the battle.

Before we can hire the best candidate and thwart discriminatory tendencies we must first understand what criteria we have for a position. For example, a manufacturing job may require enough physical strength to lift 20 pounds, a basic understanding of English, and the ability to work nights. Thus each interviewee should be ranked on their ability to fulfill these criteria. In the end the interviewer can simply take a final look at the top one or two candidates to determine a "right fit" for an organization. "Right fit" includes the right personality and outlook on business.

DIVERSITY IS PROFITS

Most business owners and executives are aware of the social impact of diversifying their workforce and encouraging a fair and equitable workplace for everyone. Yet this doesn't push diversity from a "feel good" program to one that has tangible benefits to an organization. If diversity can increase profits, reduce expenses, or help an organization to succeed there will be benefits to any organization to encourage diversity.

Diversity helps organizations to succeed by increasing customer satisfaction, reduce costs associated with training and development, and improve profits through innovation and increased sales. Thus having a diverse workforce in a global and diverse global market is a very solid business practice that few organizations can afford to ignore.

Diversity = Increased Profits = Reduced Costs

According to the 2005 Workplace Diversity Practices Survey from the Society of Human Resource Management (SHRM) a diverse workforce can reduce cost and improve profits. Responses from 400 human resource professionals indicate that 78% reported that diversity reduced costs and 74% stated that diversity improved profits.

The added benefit of increasing profits and reducing expenses is where most businesses want to be. By engaging in equitable projects companies can become more financially sound than others. Yet knowing the economic advantages of diversity doesn't tell us exactly why or how these gains are realized.

According to Richard Snead, the President and Chief Executive at Carlson Restaurants Worldwide, retention of a diversified workforce is the number one predictor of profitability and customer satisfaction (Ruggless, 2004). His organization was able to reduce turnover of its employees by 20%, which was a total savings of around $700,000 a year in training costs.

The reason why Carlson Restaurants was able to decrease training and development costs is because people of minority backgrounds felt more comfortable working in an organization that respects their uniqueness. In such organizations managers treat employees with fairness and dignity that wouldn't be available in homogeneous workplaces. In the end people are more satisfied with their work life and less likely to leave the organization.

Diversity also helps organizations to understand their customer needs better and provide better services. As customers become more diversified they prefer to deal with organizations that understand their wants and needs. By having a workforce that represents these customers' backgrounds they are more likely to provide superior service within an appropriate cultural medium.

Finally, in a globalized world companies are often represented in more than one country. A business problem in a globalized world will require a global solution. This is more likely to happen if people with *different faces, having different races from different places* are included in the solution. Thus, diversification is associated with being more innovative than monocultural companies.

DIVERSITY PAYS

Huckfeldt Herring's 2006 study, "Does Diversity Pay?: Racial Composition of Firms and the Business Case for Diversity," found that companies with racial diversity had higher sales revenues, a stronger customer base, higher profit margins, and larger market shares.

Herring states, "These results suggest that not only is having a diverse workforce a good and socially responsible thing for companies to do, but in addition, organizations that broaden their pool of qualified workers also reap material economic benefits from doing so."

According to the study average sales revenues of companies with low diversity earned on average $3.1 million, medium diversity earned $3.9 million, and high diversity $5.7 million. Similarly, high-diversity companies had an average customer base of 45,000 when compared to low-diversity companies, with 23,000. Likewise, market share of high-diversity companies was 72% when compared with 52% of low-diversity companies.

Thus it becomes easy to see that diversity is more than a "feel good" program but has a unique and worthwhile place in building strong business positions. Customers become a major issue when developing a business. Companies must have large customer bases in order to succeed. When a company hires people of different backgrounds they are able to attract a more diverse and larger customer base.

A company cannot develop a large and diverse customer base unless these customers feel comfortable dealing with company employees. For example, in the casino environment where I work, African American customers feel comfortable around African American employees, Caucasian around Caucasian, Hispanic around Hispanic, and so on. Thus diversity fosters diversity.

Diverse workforces have significant advantages over nondiverse workforces. A study by Huckfeldt Herring shows precisely why this is. Homogeneous workforces of one particular ethnic, racial, or religious background doesn't function as well as others. Take the Herring study as an example.

Huckfeldt Herring's study, "Does Diversity Pay?: Racial Composition of Firms and the Business Case for Diversity," found that businesses with greater racial diversity reported higher sales revenues, more customers, larger market shares, and greater relative profits than those with more workforces that are homogeneous.

"These results suggest that not only is having a diverse workforce a good and socially responsible thing for companies to do, but in addition, organizations that broaden their pool of qualified workers also reap material economic benefits from doing so," Herring said.

He added that racial diversity improved performance even after controlling for such factors as a firm's legal form of organization, gender composition, size, age, type of work, and region. This means that diversity has a real and not imaginary effect on the success of a company. The larger the company, the more benefits it receives from diversity.

According to his analysis, average sales revenues of organizations with low racial diversity were approximately $3.1 million, compared with $3.9 million for those with medium diversity and $5.7 million for those with high diversity.

Similarly, the average number of customers for businesses with high racial diversity was 45,525, versus 38,254 for firms with medium diversity and 23,415 for companies with low diversity.

Small companies have a difficult time realizing immediate profits from diversity mainly because they cannot achieve a wide customer base and reduce turnover that larger companies can. Such companies spend comparatively little on advertising and even less on training so they do not necessarily lose monetary value when minorities leave. Yet these companies do lose the ability to be innovative in the future. This innovation can draw a larger market share.

Companies with high racial diversity were also more likely to report higher-than-average market share (72%) and profitability (72%), compared to companies with medium diversity (66% and 61%, respectively) and low diversity (54% and 52%).

Thus diversity has a direct relationship with how much market share a company has. The higher the diversity, the more market share and visas. Any company attempting to get larger should factor the benefits of diversity into their strategy.

DIVERSITY AND SOCIETY

Diversity is also the basis of every great society. The ancient Ottomans, the Turkish, and the Americans testify that great societies allow for diversity. These societies have held the top economic and military strength for decades and only once they began to fail to keep changing did they crumble.

In the ancient Ottoman society they allowed Jewish and Christian members to rise to substantial power within the Ottoman administration. People of every background were allowed to share in the wealth of the empire and contribute to its greatness. We find that toward the end of the Ottomans' domination racism, bigotry, and brutality became the norm.

We can also look at the Romans with their brand of satellite states that brought resources back to the main headquarters. At this time the Roman Empire was extremely tolerant of Christianity and Judaism in a country where paganism was the norm. The Romans continued to grow in power until the advent of a state religion that wasn't as inclusive.

Both the Ottomans and the Romans knew the value of allowing others to share in their power and help in the decision making. By getting varying points of view the diversity brought the "buy-in" of subjected people, increase in intellectual thought, and strength in innovative technology. The empire existed for hundreds of years with few challengers.

Both in the Roman and the Ottoman world, slaves were a necessary part of life. In today's world such an institution would be seriously frowned upon but back before modern society it was as common as eating bread. Yet slavery was also considered a level of society even though it was considered the lowest. Some slaves ran large businesses, became accountants, doctors, skilled laborers, or much more. At this time it was possible for a slave to purchase his or her freedom and was often allowed to hold part-time jobs.

That does not mean that slaves were in any way considered a desired occupation or that the institution of slavery is just one, but that because the Romans allowed for "slave rights" they were able to slow down the turmoil created from constant rebellion. At this time, one could hope that they could purchase their freedom and become a full citizen in society. There are a number of cases where slaves became wealthier than their masters. The Roman society instituted hope by protecting the rights of the slave.

This of course doesn't mean that workers are slaves. Yet it does mean that rebellion, employee turnover, and participation in company objectives come from treating each employee with dignity and respect. Each employee must know that the playing field is "level" and each of them will be promoted, disciplined, and treated fairly.

When employees are treated equally and with fairness, especially diverse employees, they are more likely to stay in their current positions and work diligently for the company. That is, they have "buy-in" on company objectives and view their employers favorably.

During World War II women were forced to go to work because most of the men were out fighting the war. In the small town of Huntsville, Alabama, the Army started a chemical weapons manufacturing plant. Since most of the men who were not drafted by the Army in the 1940s were still employed in agriculture and could not devote all of their time to manufacturing, the government was forced to hire women and blacks in unprecedented ways. Other industries soon caught on to the idea of hiring women and followed suit.

It is very true that diversity did not become an important issue to business leaders and government politicians until it was absolutely necessary. While most of the able-bodied men fighting the war, women were needed to run the factories. Thus the political reality changed and a crisis was diverted by hiring women and minorities. After the war many of the women stayed working in their former newfound occupations.

From the U.S. Department of Labor we learn the following:

- 117 million women are over the age of 16 and 69 million are in the labor force.
- Women represent 47% of the U.S. labor force, of which 61.6% are black, 58.9% are white, 58.2% are Asian, and 55.3% are Hispanic.
- 75% of women worked full time while 25% worked part time.

We learn that the strong country of the United States, which has the world's largest gross national product includes women into its economy, unlike any other country in the world. Nearly half of the American economy is supported by working women and 75% of these women work full time. That means that the American economy rests in large part on the labors of women, who are an integral part of society. Even though before World War II it was uncommon and frowned upon in society for women to leave the home, the country soon learned that they had value. In today's global world many countries do not allow women to participate in contributing to their country's strength. There is very little difference between this and losing a leg while trying to win a marathon.

The history of blacks in America did not start out as a pretty picture of understanding and fair treatment. When blacks from Africa first arrived in the United States, they were treated much the same way as European immigrants. Wealthy land owners looking to find labor purchased passage tickets for immigrants and in exchange these immigrants were required to work for some prespecified time (usually 7 years) as an indentured servant. After their time in servitude they were free to roam where they wished.

Labor was hard to come by in the New World. The English satellite was separated from Europe by hundreds of miles of ocean; there were competing countries to the North and to the South, hostile Native Americans, and lots of construction and farm work available. Eventually, it became practical to simply purchase slaves instead of indentured servants. With slaves, the land owners thought they could keep them indefinitely, breed them, and tie them to the land.

Life was not easy for most slaves. Some slaves worked very hard whereas others simply sat around for hours on end with little to do. As with all people some slave owners treated their slaves well whereas others were brutal beyond description. Technically, slaves were seen as property that had no rights. They could be bought or sold, forced into sexual relationships, or even killed without so much as a discouraging glance from the government.

However, over time many land owners became forced to feed and take care of their slaves despite them having nearly no desire to do any work. Thus land owners began to abolish slavery from their plantations. They felt that if they paid workers a wage they would not be responsible for them when they got older, will get more productivity from them, and when they are no longer useful then terminate them. It certainly made more sense to hire workers whom you are not responsible for than to have slaves who would stay with you the rest of your life.

One could also look at the new immigrants to the United States. The late 1800s and the early 1900s were a difficult time for Caucasian immigrants from Germany, Italy, Ireland, and eastern Europe. The English Protestants did not feel that these groups were worthwhile to the American economy and regularly discriminated against them for their ethnic backgrounds and religious adherence (i.e., Catholicism). Over time, through changing business environments and new political realities these groups were included into the labor market to its fullest extent.

Thus the business environment has a large impact on how diversity is affected in the workplace. Just like the case of slavery or minorities the work environment did not begin to include them until after it became beneficial to do so. Thus many groups may not receive their fair share of the economy until there is some justification for including them in the spoils. As stated above there are profits to be made when diversity is included in terms of reduced turnover, a larger customer base, more innovation, and stronger management representation.

Another important aspect of diversity is "good" corporate citizenship. Companies that adhere to concepts of fair and equitable treatments with diverse backgrounds are likely to have a positive image in the marketplace. This positive image can have drastic effects on long-term growth and viability even if it isn't easily tangible.

Let us say that customers view the company as a "good" corporate citizen that represents the values of the country in which it resides. Since they feel good about the company they will also feel good about buying their products. The purchasing power of the minorities who feel the company is sympathetic to their issues as well as the larger public who respects the values of diversity is overwhelming.

There may be critics that believe that "good will" isn't really a value for a large company or organization. If you have ever heard of companies like Johnson & Johnson, Ford Motor Company, and U.S. Airways you recognize their name as synonymous with quality. This name recognition and association with quality is called "good will." The more "good will" you have, the more likely people will purchase your products because they trust you.

The U.S. government has begun to recognize "good will" as a viable value to an organization. They have thus offered it on their tax filing form SFAS 142. Nearly 100 of the largest public companies wrote off somewhere between 25–35% of their good will for tax purposes.

The new accounting rules have had a substantial effect on financial statements, as evidenced by an analysis of the 100 public companies with the largest reported good will balances. One-third of these 100 companies wrote off about 30% of their good will when they transitioned to SFAS 142.

We learn that good will is derived in part from diversification, name recognition, and good corporate citizenship. This good will has serious effects in terms of profits, monetary value, and IRS tax implications. The more noble and recognized the company, the more likely it will have a higher good-will rating.

When someone purchases a corporation or the government desires to charge taxes we find that they are conservative by nature. No one wants to pay for something that isn't real. Thus if good will were a fancy of an overpaid college professor or politician it is likely that such value wouldn't have as large of an impact in the financial world. Through experience, necessity, and common sense companies have learned that there is more to their value than the sum of their parts.

VALUES OF COMPANIES

In reality how a company treats its employees, adheres to the values of society, and treats its customers are key measures of its success. The closer the values of the organization to that held by society, the higher the likelihood the organization will be productive. The same can be said of the reverse. The difference in the values of the organization to those values held by society, the lower the worker productivity.

The reason why values are so important is because in order for companies to maintain productivity they must have the "buy-in" of their workers. The employees must feel good about the company and want to be part of the team. If the employees feel that they are not part of the team they are likely to simply do the minimum requirements of their "job" until they can move to a new company.

REFERENCES

Huckfeldt Herring's study, "Does Diversity Pay?" 2006.
Ruggles, R. (2004). Carlson Worldwide chief Snead named MUFSO Operator of Year. *Nation's Restaurant News.*
Workplace Diversity Practices Survey from the Society of Human Resource Management (SHRM), 2005.

PART IV

EMPOWERING WOMEN THROUGH EDUCATION

CHAPTER 13

VIRTUAL FACULTIES

The Education of the Future

Mirjana Radović Marković and Dučan Marković

INTRODUCTION

The development of contemporary technologies, especially the Internet, on the one hand, as well as changes in management practice, communication, and work organization in companies, on the other hand, have in recent years brought about changes in the kinds of knowledge and ways of acquiring it. In keeping with these, new educational programs have appeared, as well as new modes of studying. Among the new methods of studying, e-learning has emerged as the unquestionably most popular one, being widely accepted by both faculties opting for this method of education, and students as well. Namely, almost 90% of all American faculties offer the possibility of studying over the Internet or distance learning, thus enabling access to their study programs to all prospective students wherever they may be in terms of geographical location. Thereby faculties expand their market, and having in mind the sheer number of students at virtual faculties (more than 5 million students in the United States study at virtual faculties), Internet education is becoming one of the most profitable businesses in the world. For certain countries, such as Australia or

The Perspective of Women's Entrepreneurship in the Age of Globalization, pages 149–156

Canada, for example, Internet education has in recent years become one of the most prominent branches of the economy. Besides an exceptionally broad range of study programs offered by these faculties, they may be classified into several categories according to their method of work:

1. Virtual faculties (i.e., faculties offering online studies exclusively);
2. Traditional faculties, offering the possibility of combining face-to-face studies with e-learning. For example, within a traditional educational system, students are required to choose two or more online courses each academic year;
3. Faculties offering separate online and traditional, face-to-face studies, enabling students to choose between these.

The system of acquiring education over the Internet is year after year becoming increasingly enhanced and is improving, together with the development and improvement of Internet technologies. The development and utilization of wireless Internet has immensely contributed to the advancement of e-learning. In addition, many software packages, such as Blackboard and others, are being used. Owing to this one, as well as other pieces of software, students are enabled to be in constant contact with their virtual professors. They usually have live lectures or consultations with their professors twice a week or more often, while on other workdays professors pose questions to students, initiate discussions, send additional literature, assign topics for seminar papers, and so on. As for lectures, Yahoo voice messenger, Skype, and similar programs are used, where a professor's voice may be heard, as well as video conferencing. However, a number of faculties do not make use of such a method of communication among professors and students, but rather opt for ready-made software packages that students acquire together with the tuition fees at a certain faculty (e.g., Lacrosse University), and the student may contact the professor as need arises in the process of tackling the subject-matter coursework. At the end of the semester, the student sits for the examination, mostly administered as a test and taken online as well, and writes an independent final paper, which is defended orally.

Depending on whether the student has chosen a certified or noncertified program, he will or will not receive a diploma upon completion of the chosen study program. However, the most important fact to most students opting for studies at virtual faculties is that the diploma usually does not state the method of studies (i.e., whether the student has studied in an online or face-to-face program). The reason comes from the fact that these two methods of studies have been made completely equal in the world.

WHO IS E-LEARNING AIMED AT?

Internet studies or e-learning are aimed at all age groups across the population, one of the main reasons for its advantages, bearing in mind the fact that traditional types of studies exclude mature students. And it is the middle-age generations that have in recent years shown an increasing interest in personal and professional development, either because they had no financial resources to pursue studies at a younger age, or due to job requirements necessitating further advancement. Accordingly, there are more and more virtual faculties addressing their study programs at this market segment exclusively. Besides programs for this target group, many virtual faculties are focusing on working adults, who due to excessive workload and professional commitments cannot attend lectures on a regular basis, and find it more convenient to study from their homes at times most suitable to them. In this way they can balance their family and professional commitments more successfully, an exceptional advantage appreciated by many. Online studies are also chosen by those students who cannot afford to study abroad on account of the high costs of studying, or because they may not be granted a residence visa, but would like to acquire the knowledge and diploma of a prestigious faculty. Cases of students from Japan or any other part of the world who have studied at some of the most prestigious American, Canadian, or British universities are no longer so rare these days.

In addition to the aforementioned three target groups at which virtual faculties are aimed, they are also attractive to all those wishing to study in a comfortable way, minimizing the costs of their education at the same time.

Bearing in mind that working at virtual faculties requires new kinds of knowledge on the part of professors as well (i.e., a different approach to working with students), there are specialized programs directed at professors. Namely, professors working at virtual faculties and involved in distance learning need to have new kinds of knowledge related to the application of the state-of-the-art software packages, as well as advanced computer skills. Moreover, a professor is expected to apply a different line of approach in working and communicating with students, an aspect that should also be a subject of special training. Nevertheless, in respect to other teaching aspects, there is no difference among professors working online and those working in direct or personal contact with their students—face to face. Career advancement is pursued in the same way, and experience is a requirement for both groups of professors, as well as permanent development and other qualities pertinent to sound pedagogical work.

WHAT ARE THE ADVANTAGES OF E-LEARNING?

There have been numerous research studies into the quality and advantages of Internet education. Based on their findings, as well as personal experience in work with several similar American faculties, the following conclusions could be drawn:

1. The faculties in question offer proper studies (i.e., they offer their students contemporary, high-quality programs), updated by the semester.

2. In this way, students are, in comparison to traditional studyi methods, more motivated to make use of further literature, in addition to the one recommended or compulsory, as it is a starting point for discussion with the professor.

3. Students are encouraged to work on a systematic and regular basis rather than cram before exams.

4. Owing to the virtual communication with their professors, they are more open to discussion in comparison to traditional ways of studying.

5. This results in more efficient studying due to continuous learning, leading to the possibility of the completion of studies at an earlier date to the expected one.

6. Studying costs are considerably lowered.

7. The quality of professors' work improves, as they are required to monitor students' progress on a daily basis. Furthermore, it is an established practice at the end of the semester to perform an evaluation of each professor's efforts, and it is done by both students and the supervisor, who oversees all posts, comments, questions, and the overall activities performed by the professor. Without high marks and recommendations, a professor may not continue working and renewing his contract with the faculty. Namely, contracts are signed separately for each semester. Moreover, all professors are hired as adjunct professors, meaning that they are not provided social and pension benefits. This form of agreement reduces the faculty's costs, leading indirectly to the lowering of tuition fees, which in turn makes this form of study attractive to prospective students. Lower tuition fees significantly increase the competitiveness in comparison to traditional faculties.

8. Virtual faculties have small work groups, of 5 to 15 students. This enables a higher level of instructor commitment and possibility of better addressing students' individual needs.

9. Distance learning makes it possible to engage part-time professors working at other faculties, leading to a higher flow of fresh information, ideas, and knowledge. This in turn proves beneficial to the students.

10. A greater flexibility in program design. Namely, there is a possibility of creating specialized, personalized study programs for individual students conforming to their particular interests or needs.

11. People living in geographically distant and isolated locations, or in the countryside, far away from educational centers and leading universities, are given a chance to enroll in a desired faculty or complete a course not offered in their immediate surroundings. Thus, online studies enable students equal opportunities regarding the choice of school or studies, regardless of their place of residence.

12. Application at virtual faculties is simple and does not require much administrative work.

WHAT CAN STUDENTS EXPECT FROM VIRTUAL FACULTIES?

Most virtual faculties offer specialist, master's, and doctoral studies, being the ones that lend themselves most easily to online studies. However, there are also faculties offering full-time studies of a 3- or 4-year duration. These are slightly more difficult to organize completely over the Internet due to the high number of credits, so that those faculties putting them on their educational offerings, most often combine them with face-to-face studies. Three-year studies, which are professional career studies, are designed in such a way as to offer practical knowledge exclusively. They do not enable further continuation of studies at the post-graduate level. Unlike these, 4-year studies hold more credits, involve a combination of theoretical and practical knowledge, and as such enable the continuation of studies at the post-graduate and doctoral level. In addition to these types of studies, a number of faculties offer short courses and specialist programs. Their prices range from several hundred up to several tens of thousands of dollars depending on the duration and kind of study. However, in order for students to enroll in some of the virtual faculties, it is not sufficient to be able to afford them, but the admission requirements include the score achieved at the entrance examination. There are indicators supporting this argument (i.e., more than 80% of all students applying for admission at some virtual faculties fail in the entrance examination). Foreign students are additionally faced with taking a test of English, TOEFL, impeding them from getting enrolled. Therefore it is highly recommended to all those wishing to apply for online studies to prepare well beforehand, so as not to lose between $50 and $150, paid out for the entrance examination fee. Moreover, it is important for foreign students to complete foreign degree validation and submit it to the chosen faculties, since not all foreign schools and diplomas may be accepted. In addition, some faculties may pose special requirements regarding their prospective students (i.e., they may not allow enrollment of students from those countries listed as unwelcome according to their criteria). Therefore, there is a lot of asking around to be done before a final decision is made regarding the choice of a certain faculty or study program.

Such a strict selection of students contradicts the opinion held by some proponents of traditional studies who claim that virtual faculties are designed for making quick and easy money.

SPECIAL BENEFITS OF E-LEARNING FOR WOMEN

Distance learning is becoming increasingly attractive for women, as shown by some research studies. Namely, more than 60% of those over 25 years of age and female opt for this type of development and education in the world. The reason for this lies in the fact that this method of learning offers numerous advantages. Among the most prominent benefits, the following may be pointed out:

- the flexibility of the learning process (students study at the time most convenient to them),
- achieving a better balance between personal and other commitments (they may spend more time at home with their families),
- minimizing costs (both time and money savings are made),
- a deeper sense of self-fulfillment (acquiring relevant and useful knowledge and achieving professional goals).

Furthermore, women over the age typical for students (18–22 years of age) consider virtual classrooms to minimize the embarrassment and alienation factor. In addition to these advantages provided to women by online studying, it also enables them to choose a certified course, offered by more than 90% of faculties in the world. Accordingly, they are given the opportunity of choosing some of the programs from a broader range, the ones that best suit their professional interests and goals, without the requirement to move geographically. In other words, they are no longer limited to the local educational institutions, but have at their disposal a more comprehensive choice of educational programs offered worldwide. Also, studying over the Internet enables them permanent development, thus reducing the educational gap in comparison to men. At the same time, the social status and life quality of women are being improved. Higher qualifications enable them to contribute more to their community. A study conducted by the World Bank has recently shown that if women in the field of agriculture had the same education as men did, the agricultural yield in developing countries would increase by 6 to 22%. This example, as well as other similar ones, gives every rightful reason to focus greater attention to further development of educational programs aimed at women, but also to enhancing contemporary technologies that will improve e-learning.

CONCLUSION

Bearing in mind the aforementioned, it is reasonable to expect that online studies will continue to grow in popularity, and that the network of virtual faculties is going to keep spreading in the future. As a result, Internet education is soon going to become a dominant form of education in the world, yet to reach its peak in a few years' time. At the same time, it may be expected that methods of work and communication between professors and students will keep improving, and further efforts will be made into bettering the quality of these studies.

The degree to which a country may become integrated into the global educational Internet network will to a great extent be determined by the degree of new Internet technologies utilization and the level of popularization of this type of studies. Namely, many renowned faculties offering distance learning use famous persons enrolled in their programs as the best promoters of this kind of studies. One such campaign is led by the famous tennis player Sharapova for her faculty, where she is involved in a distance learning program, thereby contributing to its large membership due to an increasing number of prospective students interested in enrolling.

This form of education still does not have a sizable number of proponents in this country, nor are there proper Internet studies either. In other words, Internet education is still regarded as a kind of correspondence studying. In addition, many faculties are still not equipped with appropriate software and accompanying equipment for these studies, and an adequate training of staff who would be using them in their work with students is lacking as well. Besides, the development of Internet studies has not yet began life, since this country is still at the bottom of the ladder regarding the number of Internet users (abut 10%). An aggravating factor for faster development of Internet studies lies in the fact that the mindset of people here is very difficult to dislodge when it comes to embracing innovation of any kind, especially in the field of education. In line with this, most people can picture neither a "classroom without walls" nor a completely different approach to learning. For a number of people it is inconceivable not to go to the faculty, and attend lectures, since they do not feel like academic citizens otherwise. Among them, there are certainly many who are skeptical about the quality of education acquired in this way. As a result of this, although the Department of Education has included Internet education in its law, it is still in its infancy stages, and has not been given prominent media promotion. That is why this area is still relatively unfamiliar and is usually approached with a certain dose of skepticism and misgivings. In order for the existing prejudices to be overcome, it is necessary to point out to the general public the advantages of online education, so that both prospective students and their prospective employers may gain the real perspective on it. In this way, our country could also, in due time, join the company of those countries who have developed a new and profitable branch of the economy by means of a contemporary and flexible educational system. This does not mean that faculties with "classrooms without walls" will replace traditional faculties altogether. They will continue to exist and attract those students who prefer a classical way of studying, but will also need to change keeping in line with the needs and requirements of contemporary education. Therefore, it may conclude that virtual faculties and their expansion will have positive effects and influence in terms of introducing innovation at traditional faculties. It is therefore rightfully expected that besides high profits earned by faculties, the students will be the ones to benefit most, as they will receive education tailored to their wants and needs, as well as the requirements of their future workplace. This is further corroborated by data showing that in the recruitment process employers are ceasing to discriminate among applicants who graduated from Internet schools and those who completed their studies at other schools.

REFERENCES

Au, M. (1993). The evaluation of the effectiveness of various distance education methods. *International Journal of Instructional Media, 20,* 202–205.

Marković, M. R. (2006), Virtual faculties—education for the future. *Journal Radnopravni savetnik,* Poslovni biro.

Murray, S. (2006). *A new way to learn.* Available at http://www.searchenginecollege.com/articles/2006/03/new-way-to-learn-online.html

Thompson, J. (2005). *E-learning: Why choose online education?* Available at http://www.searchenginecollege.com/articles/2005/07/e-learning-why-choose-online-education.html

CHAPTER 14

COMMUNITY EDUCATION, WOMEN, AND ENTREPRENEURSHIP

Isiaka Esema

INTRODUCTION

Development is truly expressed in terms of adequacy of social amenities, very low level of poverty, or purchasing power parity (PPP) among the populace; access to healthcare delivery; and general improvement in the living standards of the people. Other indices of "true development," just like "true federalism," are visible demonstration by the people of political will through political efficacy to contribute their quota to nation-building and demonstrable community education of communitarians, particularly the community education of the most endangered species: women.

Historically, in many African nations since 150 years ago, women have been noted for serving as farm helpers for their husbands or for the household. They had very little or no education at all, they were regarded and treated as baby producers, farm hands, household keepers, or food providers for the family, but not the species that should be heard or directly involved in political affairs of their societies.

The Perspective of Women's Entrepreneurship in the Age of Globalization, pages 157–169
Copyright © 2007 by Information Age Publishing
All rights of reproduction in any form reserved.

Fortunately, for women, their roles in the home as food growers, food providers, and guardians of children really exposed them to learning how to be independent in food production as farmers/entrepreneurs who, though they lacked formal education, were well versed in community education. They knew the norms of the community, including mores, folkways, values, vices, and so on. Informally, they constitute the world's *first contact teachers for children*. This therefore explains why women's role in community education is in the fore, it also gives a finding that women are natural entrepreneurs by virtue of the way they have been treated in many African countries in the last 150 years—they can farm very well and they live more or less independent lives when it comes to providing food for the household (Kubr, 1983). Clear examples of this assertion are found in countries like India, Kenya, Ghana, Togo, Nigeria, Tanzania, Zambia, and Malawi, to mention a few.

STRUCTURE OF THE DISCOURSE

This chapter has five short sections. Section I conceptually clarifies community education and entrepreneurship as they relate to women's role in the socioeconomic development of their nation; Section II distinguishes between entrepreneurship and intrapreneurship and states the benefits of each; Section III lists the inherent qualities of a woman entrepreneur, including the constraints faced by them; Section IV spells out the strategies for effective women entrepreneurial development through sound and effective community education adverting to literature and short data, while Section V concludes the discourse on reeducation and reorientation of the minds of community leaders on the need to formally educate girls, adolescents, and women so that they can positively reshape the society through the sound moral education they will impart on children and again they will be seen to be impressing on adolescents the need to become women entrepreneurs who also financially support the home, the community, and the nation in the task of nation-building.

SECTION I. CLARIFICATION OF CONCEPTS

Community education could be defined as the process of enlightening members of the community on the norms of the community and the strategies toward ensuring positive development of the community through self-help projects, joint efforts in providing their felt-needs, and the synergistic role of all and sundry within the community.

Community education is indeed the first key to socioeconomic development. It is the subset of the economic growth and development of the community. Without real community education, which is a second-level education for a child, then communitarians cannot have their behaviors shaped by the community. Harold Laski's (1987) dictum of behaviors states that behavior is a function of environment and personality (i.e., $B = F (P \times E)$).

This means that the community (environment) in a multiplicative or geometric relationship with personality (personal lifestyle, makeup, attitude, etc., of man/woman) determines or shapes the behavior of an individual and makes him to be described as either a *deviant* or a *conformist.*

Community education therefore teaches how an individual can comport him-/herself in the community, what to do to learn the mores, folkways, subcultures, and values and how to completely go through the process of socialization in the community with emphasis on teamwork, synergy, self-help projects, and meeting other felt-needs.

Women, however, have roles to play in both informal and formal community education. Informally, women are to teach children, particularly girls, how to behave and relate with parents, cousins, peers, adults, and teachers; teach children folkways, norms, mores, and values of the community; encourage children to develop interest in teamwork, synergy, and self-help projects in order to have a good community to live in.

Formally women who are illiterates should begin to attend adult literacy classes so that they start to know how to read and write, which will usher in a realistic sense of creativity and innovation in science and technology. This will also bring out publications in community education, particularly on the strategies toward effective community education in different countries.

Entrepreneurship focuses on the individual's ability to take risks and use opportunities maximally. An entrepreneur and indeed a woman entrepreneur is one who has big eyes, big nose, large ears, big head, but small mouth. She should not talk too much or else she may reveal her business secrets, which can really get her out of business.

Although most women in Africa engage themselves at the micro level on petty trading, food vending, and nowadays they do vocations like sewing/fashion designing, hairdressing, and so on, the percentage of those who finally move into the class of entrepreneurs is very small.

In Nigeria, for example, about 27% of literate adult women constitute the cream of entrepreneurs in the country. They all started with one form of trading or the other but basically possess entrepreneurial skills such as:

- Getting the right *market* for the product.
- Getting the right *price* for the product.

- Cashing in on opportunities for growth of business.
- Effective scanning of the environment.
- Ability to take financial risks.

Being an entrepreneur is beneficial in many ways to the woman, two of these are creation of financial independence for the woman and ability to contribute meaningfully to the socioeconomic development of a country.

Community education is a process of socialization that enables members of a society to know the history of the society, the felt needs of the communitarian, the visions of the community, and how people can work in teams or groups to achieve the predetermined objectives of the community—the most important being to make the community a haven of peace and a place replete with all amenities, a much better place to live in.

A key point to stress in community education is that it is both informal and formal. Informal because the norms of the community are learned by people through corrections, reprimands, and praises for upholding ethics and values of the community. Formal in that the in-thing worldwide is to introduce written codes and written communal laws so that communitarians through their community leaders could use teachers to formally teach people (young persons and adults) on the cedes of the community.

Adults—that is, men and women who had no opportunity of schooling—could now embark on literacy programs to learn communal codes and be able to read, write, and contribute their own quota to the development of their communities.

Again, the most vulnerable set of people with little or no opportunity for community formal education is women. Taking a look at the tale above, one would see that the literacy rate of women in Nigeria in 1980 was 60.2%; in 1995 was 62.7%; and in year 2000 was 50–74% (projected).

Community education for women and the place of entrepreneurship is indeed most relevant for a discourse on the role of women in community education through entrepreneurship. A popular maxim states thus "…teach a woman then you have taught the world…" This maxim holds true because in rural communities of Kenya and Nigeria, women were seen to be the propeller of change in the way values are being appraised. Women, though with low literacy rate as given by the table above are most willing to make their children and wards become well integrated into the community and this they do through teaching the children songs, folkways, mores, dancing, plays, courtesy, and proper conduct. From all these communal interactions and other activities, women discover their true potentials and discover the entrepreneurial zeal in them, which makes them think and behave as risk takers and maximizers of opportunities available for success and progress.

By so doing, they throw themselves into real recognition as women entrepreneurs, even though they may not be completely literate. This act therefore becomes a crucial one and the very first in the bid of women's call for empowerment/ \emancipation. Through entrepreneurship, women can meaningfully contribute their own quota to their countries' socioeconomic development.

SECTION II. DISTINCTION BETWEEN INTRAPRENEURSHIP AND ENTREPRENEURSHIP INCLUDING KEY BENEFITS OF EACH

Intrapreneurship. This is a process of making an individual contribute his/her quota to the development of his/her organization or community with financial benefits/rewards so that he/she continues to look for new ways of ensuring that the objectives of the community become achieved. Intrapreneurship is an art done for the group, which attracts financial gain/benefit to the intrepreneur. The benefits are to the organization/community to the individual members of the community and to well-meaning public-spirited personalities in the society who will not prechide people from demonstrating creativity and innovativeness, which are two key concepts in developing women intrapreneurs.

SECTION III. INHERENT QUALITIES OF A WOMAN ENTREPRENEUR INCLUDING CONSTRAINTS FACED BY HER

Basically women entrepreneurs must process rare qualities to be able to become achievers and results-oriented women. Some of the qualities required by them include the following:

1. Knowledge of the environment
2. Boldness and alertness
3. Confidence
4. Average literacy to facilitate record-keeping and communication
5. Vision and penetration
6. Determination and doggedness
7. Coquetry—feminine gift of getting what they want
8. Wisdom
9. Good poise
10. Strategic focus

Some constraints faced by women entrepreneurs are:

- The fact that they are women places a cultural limitation as to the extent of visits they can make to male customers.
- Inadequate literacy levels also place a limitation on their record-keeping ability.
- A vast majority of them do not have easy access to bank loans; bank's interest rates have forced many of them to seek other sources of financial assistance to run their businesses.

SECTION IV. STRATEGIES OF DEVELOPING WOMEN ENTREPRENEURS THROUGH COMMUNITY EDUCATION

Since community education explains the process of socialization, team-work, and provision of amenities for communitarians, therefore to develop women entrepreneurs the following strategies could be utilized:

1. Registering all young and adult women who are gainfully employed in one trade or another or those who do not yet have any trade but are desirous of having one.
2. Creating a forum where women entrepreneurs would be taught "business opportunity guidance" and the A–Z of entrepreneurship for women.
3. Using a community education forum to propagate the gospel of women empowerment through engaging themselves in entrepreneurial activity.
4. Creation of funding facilities for women by government, which is also monitored and evaluated by government.
5. Organizing enlightenment programs through films, radio, and television discussions on the "woman entrepreneur."
6. Establishment of finance/investment houses by government to grant special loans with very low interest to women entrepreneurs.
7. Using the village chief (Baale) and notable women leaders to encourage women to show interest in entrepreneurship—stating the benefits.

SECTION V. CONCLUSION

Many countries in Africa and Asia still see women as household messengers; they still see them as those to fend for themselves and as the weaker sex who should not be subjected to too much rumor.

Against the backdrop of the fact that 27% of women with petty trading and other vocations finally move into a class of entrepreneurs and that many constraints abound in the way of the women entrepreneurs; it is therefore important to say that women entrepreneurs, or those aspiring to be one, must go through *a change process* that involves reorientation and reeducation. Women should actually teach workers on methods of conducting or sitting for an examination. Reorientation works on producing a virile, positive mind that tries all things successfully well. Reequation is a formal process of providing remedies to the not very good art of record-keeping, discourtesy, and not knowing business ethics and also communal ethics in business. Both reorientation and reeducation will go a long way in developing a new corps of women entrepreneurs in countries like Nigeria, Ghana, Kenya, Tanzania, and South Africa.

REFERENCES

Aina O. I. Women culture and society (Article)

Alaja-Browne, C. A. *Methods of poverty alleviation.* Paper presented at the Annual Participant's Day of Lagos State Public Service Staff Development Culture.

Ewusu, et al. (1984). *Survival strategies for rural people in Volta region of Ghana* (Article download on the Internet).

Kubr, M. (1986). *Management consulting: A guide to the profession.* Geneva: International Labour Office.

Laski, H. J. (1987). *Behaviour at work: Organizational behaviour.* New York: Groller Business Library.

TERMS OF REFERENCE

ICEA/CWRD, Lagos, Nigeria in partnership with the Liberian Ministry of Gender and Development particularly in setting up the Institute of Vocational Technology and Gender Relations, Monrovia, Liberia hereby lists out the remit/terms of Reference on the assignment as follows:

(i)   provide the platform and resource persons for a nationwide moral and civic education initiatives for schools, colleges and tertiary institutions in the Republic of Liberia;

(ii)   ensure the actualization of moral and civic education of the populace through the provision of socio-political information to government over an inte ... of two years in the first instance;

(iii)   emphasize to the citizens through the mass media the need to internalize Liberia's pledge and anthem, so that they can have a

new sense of belongingness, commitment and loyalty to the cause
of the Liberian State;

(iv)   provide the technicalities of setting-up the Liberian Institute of
Vocational Technology and Gender Relations in partnership with
the Ministry of Gender and Development Liberia;

(v)   specifically design and develop curricular for the establishment of
the under listed departments – (ref.to item b – [ii – xiii]) on the
next page;

(vi)   design and develop curricular for courses leading to the award of
first and second degree viz Bachelor and Masters;

(vii)   ensure that the institute is registered and affiliated to the University
of Liberia and Phoenix University, USA;

(viii) ensure that the institute satisfies the requirements for the award of
certificates and diplomas;

(ix)   ensure that at least two (2) donor agencies are sought to assist in
the final take-off of the Institute of Vocational Technology and
Gender Relations in Liberia;

(x)   provide interim management g..........., case studies and learning
resources including multi-media laptops and at least ten (10) computers to aid the take-off of the Institute in Liberia;

(xi)   discuss the modalities of sitting the Institute of Vocational Technology and Gender Relations, Liberia in a serene environment conducive to learning;

(xii)   discuss the cost implications of transporting facilitators from Nigeria to Liberia through a very first visit at an agreed period between
ICEA / CWRD and the Ministry of Gender Relations and Development, Liberia;

(xiii) provide a blue print of the Ideal Institute of Vocational Technology
& Gender Relations, Liberia in terms of structure costs and future
sustainability.

PROPOSALS

(a) Nationwide education for moral and civic education initiatives programmes for schools, colleges and institutions in the Republic of
Liberia.

(b) Setting up of the Institute of Vocational Technology and Gender
Relations in partnership with the Ministry of Gender & Development, Liberia.

   i.   Dept. of Women's Studies & Gender Relations.
   ii. Dept. of Fashion Designing & Textile Technology.

   iii. Dept. of Hairdressing & Barbing,
   iv. Dept. of Food & Drink Technology
    v. Dept. of Building Technology & Design.
   vi. Dept. of Transport Technology.
  vii. Dept. of Image-Making Concept, Photography, Film Production, Script Writing & Editing News Cartoon.
 viii. Dept. of Agric. & Integrated Training.
   ix. Dept. of Telecoms & Info-Technology.
    x. Dept. of Manufacturing Technology.
   xi. Dept. of Languages Communication.
  xii. Dept. of Business Management.
 xiii. Dept. of Labour Management Relations.

ASSIGNMENTS

(a) 10 years rewrite terms of conditions of Technical Assistance.
(b) Terms of Reference (Fresh).

TERMS OF CONDITIONS OF TECHNICAL ASSISTANCE

PARTNERSHIP BETWEEN
THE MINISTRY OF GENDER AND DEVELOPMENT
MONROVIA, LIBERIA

AND

INTERNATIONAL COMMUNITY EDUCATION ASSOCIATION (ICEA, LAGOS, NIGERIA / CENTRE FOR WOMEN RESEARCH AND DEVELOPMENT (CWRD), NIGERIA

ON

SETTING UP OF THE INSTITUTE OF VOCATIONAL TECHNOLOGY AND GENDER RELATIONS, MONROVIA, LIBERIA

TERMS AND CONDITIONS OF TECHNICAL ASSISTANCE

In setting up the Institute of Vocational Technology and Gender Relations, Liberia, the International Community Education Association, Nigeria in conjunction with the Centre for Women Research and Development,

Nigeria hereby adopts the underlisted terms and conditions of Technical Assistance.

PROJECT TYPE

Setting up of the Institute of Vocational Technology and Gender Relations, Liberia under the auspices of the Ministry of Women Affairs and Gender Relations, Liberia.

DURATION OF TECHNICAL ASSISTANCE

10 Years, commencing from the take-off year.

MANDATE

To organize vocational training to Liberians who already have basic education up to Secondary School Certificate level.

Other forms of training will include Seminars, Workshop and fora for adults with no formal education and workers / public servants who would like to acquire skills in various areas of callings.

ICEA/CWRD will render the following services and technically assist the Institute of Vocational Technology and Gender Relations in the areas listed below:

(a) Physical structure, equipment and facilities like tables, desks. Fans, A/C, Refrigerators, Internet hosting
- Make formal request from United Nations Development Programme to assist the Institute with the supply of 100 computers and 50 laptops with 50 LaserJet Printers and connect the Institute to the Internet.
- Make formal request from the Canadian International Development Agency (DIA) to supply 10 commoners photocopying machines.
- Suggest prototypes of buildings for the Institute of Vocational Technology and Gender Relations, Liberia. The administrative blocks will be different from the classroom blocks.
- Other facilities and equipment will be provided by the Liberian government.

HUMAN RESOURCES/FACILITATORS

ICEA/CWRD will provide at least 10 facilitators to handle different courses. The courses will be in the following areas.
- Women Studies & Gender Relations.
- Languages Communication.
- Manufacturing Technology.
- Telecommunications and Information Technology
- Image-Making Concepts.
- Labour-Management Relations.
- Agriculture / Integrated Farming.
- Transport Technology.
- Building Technology and Designs.
- Food & Drink Technology.
- Hair Dressing & Barbing.
- Fashion Design and Textile Technology.
- Business Management.

- The facilitators will travel to Liberia and hold meetings with the Ministry of Gender Relations and Women Affairs, Liberia on the modalities of getting trainees and taking-off to train the trainees and trainers later.
- The Liberian Government will provide the administrative staff of the Institute.

LEARNING RESOURCES/MEDIA TECHNOLOGY

ICEA/CWRD will bring in at least the following training equipment and learning resources namely:

- 1 Computer + 1 Printer.
- Case Studies (10) in Management.
- Management Games (5).
- 1 Multi-media Projector.
- 2 Video Tapes (Management Films).
- 2 Packets of Dri Markers.
- 2 Packets of Flip Chart Markers.
- 1 ream of Flip Charts

FUNDING AND DONOR AGENCIES

Funding will come through the following bodies:

- Liberian Government: Site, physical structure.
- Canadian International Development Agency.
- United Nations Development Programme.
- African Capacity Building Foundation, Harare: Books, Media Technology/Resources.
- Books Aid International: Books.
- British Council: Library Automations.

LEGAL SERVICES/CONTEXTS

The Ministry of Justice, Liberia will prepare legal documents for the partnership agreement and the Memorandum of Understanding (MOU) between the Liberian Government through the Ministry of Women Affairs and Gender Relations and ICEA / CWRD, Nigeria.

Other legal requirements and contexts will be provided by the Ministry of Justice, Liberia.

FUTURE SUSTAINABILITY OF THE INSTITUTE OF VOCATIONAL TECHNOLOGY AND GENDER RELATIONS, LIBERIA AND FINAL/TOTAL TRANSFER OF ASSETS, RESOURCES AND LIABILITIES BY ICEA/CWRD TO THE MINISTRY OF WOMEN AFFAIRS AND GENDER RELATIONS, LIBERIA

- The ICEA / CWRD will act as foster body for the Institute of Vocational Technology and Gender Relations for a period of seven (7) years, thereafter all assets, resources and liabilities will be totally and finally transferred to the Institute.
- The Institute will go into Revenue Generation activities such as letting out of halls, etc.
- The Institute will get funded by Donor Agencies e. g. Books Aid International, British Council—for books and library automation.

AFFILIATIONS

- University of Liberia, Monrovia.

- University of Ibadan, Nigeria.
- Administrative Staff College of Nigeria, Topo, Badagry, Lagos, Nigeria.
- University of Phoenix, USA.
- University of Pretoria, South Africa.
- University of British Columbia, Canada.
- United Nations International Institute for the Advancement of Women, Santa, Dominican Republic.

COST IMPLICATIONS (RESOURCE PERSONS)

ICEA/CWRD will in the interim provide 10 resource persons to deploy training in the following areas:

- Training and Development
- Human Resources Management
- Telecoms & InfoTech.
- Manufacturing Technology
- Science and Technology
- Agriculture & Integrated Farming
- Transport Technology
- Women Studies and Gender Relations
- Labour Management Relations
- Business Administration
- Management
- Language Arts
- Building Technology
- Image-Making Concepts
- Food & Drink Technology
- Textile Technology
- Hairdressing & Barbing

INCONVENIENCE ALLOWANCES FOR 7 DAYS
(MONDAY–SUNDAY)

(a)	$10 \times \$1000 \times 7$	70,000
(b)	Accommodation for 6 nights for 10 people—$10 \times \$1500$	90,000
(c)	Airfare to and from Liberia/Nigeria for 10 people	70,000
(d)	Return ($700.00)	

CHAPTER 15

ENSURING QUALITY FOR NONTRADITIONAL UNIVERSITIES AND COLLEGES

Douglass Capogrossi

INTRODUCTION

There has been a growing trend for mid-career adults to return to the arena of higher education. Increasingly, these returning students seek opportunities to avail themselves of the broad array of learning resources of a university community, without seriously impacting upon their employment and family responsibilities. Many flock to programs for advanced study that provide flexible arrangements of time, residency, study options, application of knowledge, and integration with career activities. Students living in remote locations or isolated by disability and incarceration seek opportunities for study appropriate to their limiting arrangements. For adult students, nontraditional alternatives have become increasingly popular.

In response to the emerging demand for college alternatives, traditional and new nontraditional programs have sprung into existence, some providing popular alternatives to the campus environment. Accrediting associations and government ministries worldwide have adjusted policies and oversight to address these emerging models of education, to avoid any

The Perspective of Women's Entrepreneurship in the Age of Globalization, pages 171–176
Copyright © 2007 by Information Age Publishing
All rights of reproduction in any form reserved.

overall weakening of educational quality standards. These accreditors seek to ensure that nontraditional institutions are addressing the needs of the learner in a worthy manner, through high standards of quality and integrity and effective models of education. This chapter examines the academic literature and reflects upon the relevance of the findings for nontraditional education.

THE DEMANDS OF QUALITY

Developing an analytical disposition along with the skills of critical thinking among students is an almost universal aim among university professors. It is known that mentorship, such as the educational model perfected by contemporary institutions like Akamai University, is believed to be an effective instructional model, adding important elements not included in earlier models of distance education. This delivery model, one-on-one mentorship, is determined to be more effective at providing necessary feedback to students, increasing student study interests, and in promoting critical independent thinking. Mentorship is capable of more clearly presenting and explaining the subject matter, and in helping students understand the theories, principles, and practices presented in the coursework. Consequently, educational institutions that use mentorship effectively are capable of instilling in their students a questioning, critical attitude accepted as one of the hallmarks of higher education (Au, 1993, p. 108).

Research shows that autonomous learners pursuing individualized programs of study, on their own initiative, learn both from themselves and from others, establishing a relationship of mutuality between themselves and their learning environment. Over the years, student autonomy has become associated with concepts such as self-responsibility, helping learners assume accountability for their own learning, and self-determination, based on a perception of needs and interests. Mature individuals, able to reflect in detail upon their professional field and the academic literature of the subject matter, have high potential to become accomplished autonomous learners.

Although independent learning may run contrary to the more traditional accredited classroom-based models, in that faculty are less in control of the primary learning environment, the academic literature recognizes that as students move toward autonomy, the teacher should remain in authority but transition progressively less in authority and more as a facilitator, as the student skills develop. Structures and boundaries must remain as features of the learning system but aspects of these should be less imposed and more negotiated. A successful teacher of the effective autonomous learner combines the roles of manager, facilitator, and resource person without excessively imposing their wills upon their students (Elton, 1988, pp. 219–220).

The weight of evidence from traditional experimental studies further supports approaches that individualize instruction, showing them to be reasonably more effective at improving the acquisition of subject-matter content over more conventional subject matter approaches such as the traditional lecture and discussion. This learning advantage appears to occur without giving rise to undesirable side effects in terms of negative student attitudes toward instruction, increased withdrawal rates, or increased time required to meet course demands (Pascarella & Terenzini, 1991, pp. 89–93).

It appears that students experience the most effective outcomes when they are involved in identifying learning needs, setting goals, planning learning activities, finding resources for learning, working collaboratively with colleagues, selecting and defining learning projects, and creating problems to tackle. These more effective processes allow students to choose where and when they will learn, using teachers as guides, mentors, and counselors rather than mere instructors, and permitting them to reflect upon the learning process, and make significant decisions about these matters (Lewis, 1988).

The research literature provides additional support for effectiveness of guided independent learning models and concludes that in addressing individual needs of adult learners, attention must be paid to adaptability. The innovation of combining distance learning with individualized study plans serves genuinely academic ends, enhancing the learning of facts and fundamentals, and acquisition of skills. Unlike outcomes of distance education alone, adding program adaptability relieves the danger of merely transmitting facts and opinions at the lower levels of cognition. When adult students are encouraged to search for facts within the details, relationships, problems, and solutions on their own, they perform a truly effective academic activity (Holmberg, 1992, p. 12).

Perhaps the greatest departure from traditional education through individualized distance learning is its explicit recognition that education should be measured by what students know rather than how or where they learn it (Perraton, 1982, p. 7). During the late 1980s, with the support of the Fund for Advancement of Education, a number of colleges experimented with large programs of independent study. They found few differences between achievement of students working independently and those taught in conventional classrooms (Holmberg, 1992, p. 11).

The value of independent study, however, is greatest for the adult learner of high capability with a good deal of background in the area to be covered, since this student will be less likely to be overwhelmed by the difficulties commonly encountered in such studies (McKeachie, 1986, p. 143).

This factor makes it clear that the student audience for colleges and universities conducting programs by autonomous learning methods must be mature, academically and professionally, in their desired fields of study. Graduate-level programs and final-year undergraduate programs that serve mid-career adult students are most effective at satisfying this expectation.

It is also understood that truly effective outcomes are possible when the mode of instruction demands that the student establish an effective project-oriented learning environment. This requires the student to have a viable learning laboratory whereby they may interface with their professional arena through true-to-life interactions and challenges. Under such conditions, faculties are free to coach their students to view learning as an active process over which they should take initiative and exercise a great deal of control. The focus overall is to be placed upon moving student learning to higher levels of cognition, whereby they are expected to create and evaluate, do independent original thinking, make judgments, communicate unique ideas, feelings, and experiences, and design effective solutions to "real-life" situations. The nature of this type of outcome is contributory to the development of effectiveness for mid-career adults, building competencies useful in securing career achievements (Capogrossi, 2002).

BUILDING QUALITY INSTITUTIONS

A worthy institution will view quality issues as primary and integral throughout the conceptual design, delivery, and follow-up of its education programs. Quality institutions govern their curriculum, instruction, and support services by policies and standards established to ensure future success of the participants (Capogrossi, 2002). For instance, successful institutions will design their learning objectives to serve the demonstrated needs of the desired student audience. The academic and professional needs of that audience will be at the foundation of the curriculum and the subject-matter objectives will become the focus of the quality control process. The assessment and examination vehicles will evaluate student knowledge and competencies measured against learning objectives derived from the needs of industry and the professions.

Performance standards for faculty will highlight effectiveness in delivery and will address shortcomings in a timely manner. Instructional staffs are carefully selected for effectiveness in preparation, commitment to the discipline, and professional excellence. Successful nontraditional colleges will grant admittance to self-directed adults having the requisite maturity and academic capabilities. Faculty leadership monitors the professional arena of the student body, identifying the changing needs for education and training. These elements are interpreted and translated in establishment of entry requirements and continuous upgrading of curriculum.

Quality nontraditional universities ensure adequacy in the resources available for student learning. Such resources must ensure access to theories, principles and practices, and advanced concepts that underscore each program of study. To ensure the institution achieves a high standard of quality in the selection of learning resources, the institution will assign qualified faculty and academic librarians to decide upon effective study materials, textbooks, and library resources.

Effective nontraditional institutions ensure students achieve high-level abilities to interpret the writings and research of scholars and make maximum use of the literature in application of their chosen discipline. Students analyze and summarize the essence of the scholarly literature and report to their professional colleagues, integrating new learning within their professional setting.

The nontraditional university establishes and monitors policies, protocols, standards, and guidelines for the conduct of effective student research. It ensures that quality faculty members who are experienced academic researchers oversee and control quality in experimental, applied, and philosophical research and inquiry.

CONCLUDING REMARKS

Nontraditional education achieves cognitive outcomes equal to those achieved by more traditional means of educational delivery for adults. Additionally, distance learning has advantages over more traditional strategies when learning is closely aligned and related to the reality of life and work, such as under conditions where students remain fully engaged with their professional lives while under the mentorship of qualified academics. This association of academic projects with the work situation of the student permits effective integration of new learning within the workplace of the practitioner. This form of outcome, applied and integrated, differs greatly from simply providing disconnected sets of theories and principles, no matter how well organized the presentation.

A high-quality nontraditional approach requires that the educational institution treat knowledge more open-endedly, permitting students to theorize for themselves, giving them greater access to the data, greater responsibility and freedom, and the opportunity to engage in critical thinking, matching theories against available data. Integration of knowledge pursued by students alone is likely to be more meaningful than integration done for them. Engaging the adult student in creating and evaluating knowledge is a vital factor that justifies the integration of mentorship, independent study, and external projects, since such activities engage the adult students in organizing their own knowledge, rather than simply storing the inferences and appropriate sets of data that were put together by the experts.

If an essential goal of higher education is to help students develop the ability to continue learning after the formal education is complete, it seems reasonable that they should have a good deal of supervised experience in learning independently. This may be carried out through experiences in which qualified faculty mentors help the adult student formulate problems, find answers, and evaluate their progress themselves.

AUTHOR'S NOTE

A different version of this concept is previously published in the *Journal of Higher Education in Europe, 27,* No. 4.

REFERENCES

Au, M. (1993). The evaluation of the effectiveness of various distance education methods. *International Journal of Instructional Media, 20*(2), 105–126.

Capogrossi, D. (2002). The assurance of academic excellence among nontraditional universities. *Journal of Higher Education in Europe, 27*(4), 481–490.

Ellton, L. (1988). Conditions for learning autonomy at a distance. *Programmed Learning and Educational Technology. 3.*

Holmberg, B. (1992). Innovatory approaches serving or threatening academic excellence—An international concern. *International Journal of Innovative Higher Education, 8,* 12

Lewis, R. (1988). Do correspondence students need counseling? *Distance Education, 1*(2), 142–162.

McKeachie, W. (1986). *Teaching tips: A guidebook for the beginning college teacher.* Lexington, MA: D.C. Heath.

Pascarella, E., & Terenzini, P. (1991). *How college affects students.* San Francisco: Jossey-Bass.

Perraton, H. (1982). *The cost of distance education.* Cambridge, International Extension College.

Stewart, D. W., & Spille, H. A. (1988). *Diploma mills: Degrees of fraud.* New York: ACE/ Macillan.

Syllabus [Editor] Interactive Media. (2002). An interview with Chris Dede (Harvard University). *Syllabus: Technology for Higher Education, 15,* No. 11.

CHAPTER 16

WOMEN IN DISTANCE EDUCATION IN NIGERIA

Eugenia Onwu Ukpo

INTRODUCTION

"My religion and tradition does not allow mixing male and female in one place. Look at Qur'anic schools—males and females are separated; so how can I allow my grown up daughter to be seated side-by-side with a mature man and expect nothing to happen?" (*Daily Trust*, October 6, 2006, p. 42)

Overcoming deep-seated sociocultural, political, and economic barriers that have helped create gender disparities in access to education mostly in African countries is particularly critical, if Education for All (EFA) and the Millennium Development Goals (MDGs) are to be achieved by 2015. Discrimination in gender roles against girls and practices such as early marriage and childbearing often leads to girls dropping out of school, especially girls from poor homes in the northern region of Nigeria. Although Universal Basic Education (UBE) was launched in 1999, the education of the girl-child still lags behind that of boys. UNICEF projections based on attendance data for 81 developing countries show a gender parity index (GPI) of 0.92 in 2005 for Nigeria. This means that there are 92 girls for every 100 boys in primary school. Nigeria is therefore one of the countries that failed to meet the target date set for achieving MDG 3 by 2005.

The Perspective of Women's Entrepreneurship in the Age of Globalization, pages 177–184
Copyright © 2007 by Information Age Publishing
All rights of reproduction in any form reserved.

In order to enable women to redefine their private and public roles, a change in the status of women has been placed at center stage by the political leadership in a reform agenda of social transformation of Nigerian society. Within this reform agenda, a number of policy initiatives have been instituted by the Federal Government through the Federal Ministry of Education to facilitate and ensure access to education for girls. One such initiative is the Strategy for the Acceleration of Girls Education (SAGEN), which was launched in collaboration with UNICEF in 2003. Within the framework of SAGEN is the Girls Education Project (GEP), launched in 2004. GEP is a joint initiative of the Federal Government of Nigeria, the Department for International Development (DfID), and UNICEF, which is being implemented in 15 states of northern Nigeria, starting in six states (Borno, Sokoto, Niger, Bauchi, Jigawa, and Katsina) in the first phase, 2005–2007.

In addition, distance education is being used as a strategy for widening participation in education. Although distance education has not been particularly targeted at only women, many have taken advantage of it. This chapter aims to look at women enrollment trends in distance education programs in Nigeria, with particular reference to distance teacher education programs and how women distance learners can be supported to successfully complete their studies.

DISTANCE EDUCATION IN NIGERIA

Open and distance learning, because of its cost and delivery characteristics, is and has been seen as a viable means of providing educational opportunities for minority and disadvantaged groups who cannot attend conventional educational institutions. This form of education has been defined by Keegan (1990) as distinct from other forms of education by five characteristics, namely:

- The quasi-permanent separation of teacher and learner throughout the length of the learning process (this distinguishes it from conventional face-to-face education);
- The influence of an educational organization both in the planning and preparation of learning materials and in the provision of student-support services (this distinguishes it from private study and teach-yourself programs);
- The use of technical media—print, audio, video, or computer—to unite teacher and learner and carry the content of the course;
- The provision of two-way communication so that the student may benefit from or even initiate dialogue (this distinguishes it from other uses of technology in education); and

- The quasi-permanent absence of the learning group throughout the length of the learning process so that people are usually taught as individuals and not in groups, with the possibility of occasional meetings for both didactic and socialization purposes.

Before the term *distance education* was officially adopted in 1982, a number of Nigeria's educated elite had benefited from the University of London through correspondence studies. For instance, E.O. Ajayi and Alvan Ikoku, both prominent Nigerians, were reported to have obtained the University of London degrees in philosophy between 1927 and 1929 (Omolewa, 1985). Even after the establishment of the University College in Ibadan, in 1948, many Nigerians still continued to enroll for higher learning programs through the University of London as distance learners. Today, a number of institutions offer distance education programs. These institutions include:

1. The National Teachers' Institute (NTI) established in 1976 as the only single-mode distance education institute to among other things provide courses of instruction leading to the development, upgrading, and certification of teachers.

2. The Ahmadu Bello University Correspondence and Teachers' In-Service Programs, established in 1976.

3. The Correspondence and Open Studies Unit of the University of Lagos established in 1974.

4. The National Open University of Nigeria, which enrolled its first students in 2003, is also a single-mode university.

5. Private organizations and professional bodies also provide distance learning courses in areas such as law, business administration, and accounting.

Through these institutions, distance education has contributed immensely to educational growth and development in the country. One area in which it has contributed the most is in the production of teachers to cope with the demand, particularly in the basic education subsector. The NTI currently runs three teacher training programs: Nigeria Certificate in Education (NCE), Post Graduate Diploma in Education, and Advanced Diploma courses in Early Childhood Education and school supervision.

WOMEN DISTANCE LEARNERS IN NIGERIA

Different types of students make use of distance education. In most cases they are adults, whose ages range from 20 to 40. Data on the participation of women in distance education in Nigeria is not easy to obtain, as there is no central database for distance education. Second, it is difficult to access the scale of distance education provision in the country as there are many conventional institutions also offering this form of education. However, female students form an increasingly diverse group within the distance education population in the country, both in terms of their demography and the type of courses they pursue.

Olakulehim and Ojo (2006) have classified women distance learners in Nigeria into four broad categories. The first are full-time housewives who have never had access to formal education or who had to give up school at early stages of their lives. Women in this category have their children and/ or other dependants to care for and therefore are unable to travel away from home to attend conventional institutions. The second groups are women in *Purdah* (a practice that isolates women from public observation among Muslims). There are also women in full-time employment, who have only a college degree and want to further their education. The final groups are the nomadic women. Distance education is considered suitable for all these groups because they can study from home.

Although Nigerians have benefited from distance education for more than two decades, it is in the area of teacher education that distance education has found its greatest application. There is generally a high participation rate for women, particularly in the teaching profession in Nigeria. In Colleges of Education, female enrollment has increased steadily over the years. For example, out of a total number of 151,578 students registered in 2001 for the Nigeria Certificate in Education (NCE) program run by Colleges of Education, 80,876 (53%) were female (Isyaku, 2003). In 1990, when the NTI NCE by distance learning started, 78% of the 29,214 students enrolled in the program were female. Although regional disparities exist with the Northern States having lower female enrollment, females are still clearly in the majority in the NTI program, as reflected in Table 16.1.

WOMEN'S SUPPORT NEEDS IN DISTANCE EDUCATION

Learner support in distance education focuses on providing learners with the assistance they need to achieve their desired outcomes in a distance-learning environment. As already mentioned above, the high enrollment of females in distance education is an indication that this mode of education is more suitable or attractive for them, considering their usually busy domestic lives. Nevertheless, these advantages are not always guaranteed.

Effeh (1991) and Bhalalusesa (2001), for example, focus on the problems faced by women undergoing distance education programs in Africa

TABLE 16.1
Proportion of Men and Women in NTI NCE distance learning Program, 2001–2005

Year	Total students	Men (%)	Women (%)
2001	56,375	41.8	58.2
2002	71,714	40.4	59.6
2003	89,150	41.7	58.3
2004	93,547	40.0	60.0
2005	91,259*	38.0	62.0

* Out of 91,259, enrollment for women in the Northern States was 20.2% against 41.7% in the South.

Source: Compiled from the NTI Annual Reports for the period 2001–2005

and suggest that it is particularly difficult for women in this part of the world, where the patriarchal nature of society has the tendency of impacting negatively on women's educational endeavors. Due to the negative stereotyping in Nigeria (e.g., educated women do not respect their husbands or do not reflect the local culture in their mode of dressing), support is more likely to be forthcoming to males within the partnership than to females. This highlights the particular plight of women returning to study. Again, Kirup, and von Prümmer (1997) have questioned the universal notion of "independent" and "autonomous" learner, which has dominated the literature on distance education. Although the authors' studies were based on European women, their suggestion that the notion of the "connected" learner is most suited to women's learning styles; since more female than male distance education students suffer from the isolation of studying at a distance, is applicable to many cultures, including Nigeria. This explains why it is important to provide access to some form of communication with the providing institution, not only to humanize their studies and help them feel valued, but also to enable them to establish a strong identity within such institutions.

Apart from isolation and the need for social interaction, money to pay for their fees is another main worry for most women. In Nigeria as in most African cultures, it is preferable for the husband to study since his achievement is regarded as an achievement for the entire family. As a result, any funds available are spent on running the home rather than sending the woman to school. Financial support for the woman is therefore crucial for her to successfully complete her studies.

CURRENT SUPPORT FOR STUDENTS STUDYING AT A DISTANCE IN NIGERIA

Most distance learning institutions in the country provide one form of learner support services or the other. Historically, the NTI has used a decentralized support system and the type of support offered has been directed to both male and female students. Four categories of learner support are currently being offered. These include:

1. *Tuition.* This is by correspondence through printed texts. The main strategy is the provision of self-instructional course materials that contain course content. The modules are in the form of self-contained learning materials, which is supplemented by face-to-face contact sessions aimed at establishing contact between learners and tutors and learners and learners. Tuition also includes correspondence-based strategies, meant to provide immediate feedback to students such as commenting on and grading tutor-marked assignments (TMAs).

2. *Counseling services.* Orientation for new students, preregistration counseling, preexamination briefing, print-based strategies built into the students' handbook (e.g., study guide advising students on when/ where to study, how to study a unit/how much to study per week, materials required for study), bulletins, circulars, and newsletters.

3. *Community resources.* Study space (e.g., study centers), facilities for conduct of practical, schools for practice teaching, and library services.

4. *Administrative support.* Information services, responding to routine enquiries/queries, processing admission, record keeping, delivering course materials, and program monitoring.

Apart from the support strategies mentioned above, the NTI also produces audio/videocassettes as support materials for students. To cater for students' needs, the NTI has designed into its distance learning programs connection networks that facilitate face-to-face student-to-student contact, as well as student–tutor contact. The Institute has about 345 NCE study centers (NTI, 2005), spread all over the country, where students meet for tutorials on weekends and during school holidays. Both male and female students are encouraged to attend contact sessions. Although support is provided for both males and females, my experience and contact with students reveal that women have the tendency to form their own study groups and support networks. They also tend to value the support from their families more. Evidence from a recent study showed that their success on the NTI course depended not only on the role of the Institution, but also on the support from their families (Ukpo, 2005).

CONCLUSION

Open and distance learning (ODL) from the experiences of many countries has been seen to offer the most cost-effective means, when compared to conventional education of providing opportunities for greater access to education. Due to certain distinct advantages that make it suitable, particularly in the changing global educational context, it is potentially better placed to move the country forward in providing education for all and achieving the MDGs. Although there are no distance education initiatives specifically targeted at women at the moment, women in Nigeria have recognized the potential for distance education to help them redress their educational disadvantage, and the enrollment figures in teacher education are very optimistic.

This chapter has highlighted a number of issues that need to be considered to ensure that women distance learners in Nigeria are being given the support they need to succeed. These issues lead to the following conclusions in using distance education to provide access to educational opportunities for women.

- Women in distance education do need support to learn successfully. The support can come from various sources: the institution providing the learning opportunity, families and friends, the immediate social environment/community, and fellow students.
- There is a need for attitudinal change towards women's education in Nigeria. This can be achieved through sensitization programmes and awareness campaigns, using drama, posters and radio jingles.
- The need to provide financial support for women who have embarked on successful study.
- Providing educational opportunities targeted at women, and documenting the experiences of women who have successfully completed a course of study to serve as role models for other women.

Addressing the issues outline above will help to enhance the quality of distance education experience for women in Nigeria.

REFERENCES

Ahmed, S. (2006, October 6). Girl-child education in Kebbi. *Daily Trust,* p. 42.

Bhalalusesa, E. (2001). Supporting women distance learners in Tanzania. *Open Learning, 16*(2), 155–168.

Effeh, E. (1991). Determinants of the study patterns of female distance learners: An evaluative survey. *Journal of Distance Education, 1*(2), 58–63.

Isyaku, K. (2003, July). *Revitalising teaching in Nigeria*. Paper presented at a Symposium on the Future of Nigerian Education, Teddington Lock, United Kingdom.

Keegan, D. (1990). *Foundations of distance education* (2nd ed.). London: Routledge.

Kirup, G., & Von Prummer, C (1997). Distance education for European women: The threats and opportunities of new educational forms and media. *European Journal of Women's Study, 4*(1), 39–62.

NTI. (2005). *Annual Report*. Kaduna: NTI Press.

Olakulein, F. K., & Ojo, O. D. (2006). Distance education as a women empowerment strategy in Africa. *Turkish Online Journal of Distance Education, 7*(1), 13.

Omolewa, M. (1985). Origins and development of distance education in Nigeria. *Nigerian Educational Forum, 8*(2), 143–149.

Ukpo, E. O. (2005). *Learner support in distance education: A mixed method evaluation of the National Teachers' Institute (NTI) Nigeria Student Support System*. Unpublished EdD dissertation, University of Bristol, Graduate School of Education.

CHAPTER 17

MUSLIM WOMEN EDUCATION IN KENYA

Najwa Gadaheldam

LOW LEVEL OF MUSLIM EDUCATION

Muslims in Kenya predominantly occupy Coast Province, North Eastern, and the Northern part of Eastern Province. Muslims are also found in all the remaining provinces such as Nairobi, Central, Western, Nyanza, and Rift Valley in the minority form.

From 1920–1963, the Kenya education system was divided into government and religious schools, for example, there were education systems for Europeans, Asians, Arabs (Hindus, Sikhs, Shahs, Ismaili, Muslims), and Africans. From 1964 to date, there are still public and private secular educational institutions. Public primary schools cater to children ages 6–14 years of all religious denominations throughout the country. However, some schools still bear the names traceable to the religious faiths that established them.

For example, there are the Aga Khan Schools for the Ismaili Muslims, Guru Nanak, the Swaminarans, Muslims, and Christian schools. We have Visa Oshwal for the Shahs and Precious Blood Schools and Our Lady of Mercy Catholic Schools (for girls) and other church schools such as Baptist, Methodist schools, colleges, and universities in the country. Some of

The Perspective of Women's Entrepreneurship in the Age of Globalization, pages 185–195
Copyright © 2007 by Information Age Publishing

these schools still have strong religious beliefs, and a lot of their programs are religious (i.e., Christian).

These Christian-based institutions are overcrowded by Christian students, and the Muslim students in these colleges are a minority. Muslim students in these Christian-based schools and colleges have difficulty in accessing mosques where they can pray on Fridays. Secondary schools in Kenya have a school timetable running from Monday morning to Friday evening. This arrangement does not allow Muslim students time to attend prayers on Fridays, as their faith demands. Another constraint to the Muslim girls education in secondary schools is that all girls must be dressed in school uniform during the school days; this rule does not permit Muslim girls to dress in veils and scurf. It is believed that such rigid rules in Kenyan secular secondary schools tend to push some Muslim girls out of educational institutions.

There are many additional factors that affect Muslim education in Kenya. In this case, the educational planners need to study fully how to integrate Muslim students into the secular education system. It is understood that Muslims all over the world, including those in arid and semi-arid lands in Kenya such as North Eastern Province, are literate and educated in the Arabic language, both in writing and reading of the Koran, after the age of 7 years. This is said to be true because of household-level institutionalization of the Madrassa or Duksi system of education within the Muslim communities and in the mosques. The current low level of participation of Muslims in secular education in Kenya can be attributed to the highly Christianized secular education by the missionary churches from Europe.

In the present secular education in Kenya children from pre-primary education programs or the Early Childhood Education Programs start at the age of 3–5 years before joining standard one (Grade One) then start primary education at the age of 6 years. At this time in the life of Muslim children, they must "Hitimu," that is, to satisfy their Madrassa/Duksi instructors, that they have satisfactorily attained the levels required in Arabic/Koran tutelage, before they are released to their parents to take them to the secular schools for Early Childhood Education Development (ECD) and later to primary school Grade One admission. If the scenario described above has to work, it means a Muslim child is likely to join Grade One primary school education at the age of 10 years, while the non-Muslim children are joining these secular schools at the age of 6 years, because ECD education programs take 2–3 years, and this conflicts with Madrassa schooling.

When the Muslim girls get to this age, it is only a couple of years before they get married off by their parents at the age of 14 years. This situation calls for the need to provide an integrated curricular education at Madrass/Duksi/ECD level to cater to Muslim children. It is understood that Muslim mothers are extremely reluctant to release their daughters to attend co-educational secular primary schools, where boys mix freely with girls. This situation is calling for either girls-only or boys-only schools both in rural and urban areas, which are not readily available in Muslim-dominated rural districts, and are also very scarce even in urban areas, with pockets of Muslim populations.

Cultural norms, values, beliefs, and occupational status preferences also tend to keep Muslim youth away from education and training systems. Some training opportunities lead to performing certain occupations; Muslims living in the Northern part of Kenya may be interested in doing certain jobs, while Muslims living along the Coastal region may be interested in different occupations.

It is imperative to undertake needs assessment in the Muslim areas to identify what type of courses or occupations they prefer. There are efforts in Kenya at the moment to integrate Madrassa/Duksi education with ECD curriculum as one way of improving education of Muslim children within ages 3–10 years in primary education.

With the support of donor organizations such as UNICEF, Muslim role models are being used to campaign to promote education and training for Muslim girls and women in Kenya. A group of academically qualified and trained personnel in education and other occupations are currently busy traversing the districts in the large Muslim population areas in the Coast, Eastern, and North Eastern Provinces in an effort to promote education for all Muslim children in general.

These challenges enumerated above, together with others that have been addressed in this chapter, are the causes of the low level of education in Kenya for the Muslim children, particularly girls.

YOUTH POLYTECHNICS TRAINING INSTITUTIONS

"According to the United Nations, Universal Declaration of Human Rights Article 23, Everyone has the right to work, to free choice of employment, to just and favorable conditions of work and protection against unemployment."

Recognizing this right to all Kenyans, the National Council of Churches of Kenya (NCCK) in 1968 noted that formal school was turning out thousands of primary school levers who share high job expectations but are ill-equipped to pursue formal or self-employment. Thousands of youth caught in this flocked into towns in search of nonexistent jobs. The Youth Polytechnics were planned to equip the local youth in their villages with Vocational Skills to enable them to enter self-employment in the informal sector of the economy. There aims were that:

- Youth Polytechnics were to provide their trainees with the knowledge, skills, and attitudes that will lead them into income-generating activities in the areas where they live.
- The youth will learn to use their skills and talents for improving the standards of living in their communities in which they live and hence stem out rural-to-urban migration.

Over 60% of the world lives in rural areas where the youth need local employment opportunities to build their communities and stem out rural-to-urban migration. Kenya realized that the youths are the most important resources in agriculture and rural employment creation. In a developing country such as Kenya, there is hardly any growth in jobs creation in both public and private sectors.

According to the Permanent Secretary, Kenyan Ministry of state for Youth Affairs Mr. Kinuthia N. Murugu stated, "Young people every where face numerous challenges as they make their transition from adolescence to adulthood, and finally mature in adulthood. In Kenya as in many other developing countries, access to employment and economic opportunities that enable the youth to earn an honest and descent livelihood is probably the most fundamental of the challenges."

Failure to access these opportunities makes the young people dependant and ultimately undermines their self-esteem. Leaving young people out of the economic mainstream is, however, a national tragedy. In a country like Kenya, which is not endowed with many natural resources, this robs this society of its most energetic, dynamic, and innovative resources.

THE AIMS OF YOUTH POLYTECHNIC PROGRAMS

The main objectives of Youth Polytechnic programs in Kenya are:

- To impart relevant vocational and business (entrepreneurship) skills for self-employment in the learner.
- To influence the attitudes of the youth to embrace manual work and business enterprises as viable employment opportunities for earning a decent living. Lack of employment leads to lack of income to an individual, hence the increase of poverty in the society.

The planners in the government should not allow youth unemployment to continue at the current crisis proportions. This trend must be halted and reversed through youth enterprises development strategies. The status of economic activities in ASAL areas of Kenya centered on livestock farming and crop production for domestic use, in an environment affected with poor rainfall and an inadequate and poorly developed infrastructure, a high level of poverty, an acute shortage of food and water, high levels of illiteracy, and school dropout problems.

The ASAL areas have no developed industrial setups to create off-the-farm employment opportunities. The only hope for the idle youth in these areas is to venture into enterprise development work activities, which could include value -added production, agro-business, livestock trade, cooperatives, veterinary services, environmental work activities, house construction, and rural road construction work for the purpose of generating income for youth.

There is a well-developed Micro and Small Enterprises (MSEs) Sector in Kenya, which provides one of the prolific sources for employment opportunities, not to mention one of its roles as the breeding ground for medium and large-scale industries, which are critical for industrialization of the country. The current MSE sector in Kenya contributes 18.5 % of GDP, while employing over 6 million persons.

ACCESS TO VOCATIONAL SKILLS AND TECHNOLOGY FOR MSE SECTOR ACTIVITIES

The prerequisite to improve MSEs sector production quality and competitiveness is access to modern and appropriate technology know-how. Technology development in any business undertaking depends on the level of technology knowledge of the entrepreneurs in that particular line of business he or she is doing. One of the objectives for setting up the Youth Polytechnics is to impart relevant vocational skills to the learners for self or wage employment opportunities in the rural or urban areas. The ASAL areas need much more Youth Polytechnics than those already established to absorb the increasing number of primary school leavers in the areas, in training them for self-employment.

The latest statistics available indicate that currently there are 697 Youth Polytechnics, spread throughout the country, of which 395 are receiving government assistance and the remaining 302 are owned and run by the private sector, religions, and communities. A number of Youth Polytechnics have received assistance from many organizations, including the private sector, development partners, NGOs, and other well wishers.

REVITALIZATION OF YOUTH POLYTECHNICS TRAINING INSTITUTIONS

With the rapid technological development and globalization of the industrial and commercial sectors of the economy, coupled with the changing trends in national goals, policies, and objectives of the current Youth Polytechnics and other similar vocational training sectors, have to be refocused with clear policies, objectives, and implementation strategies in order to:

- Provide education and vocational training that promotes vertical and horizontal mobility and relevant skills for the current job market.
- Manage the current challenges and exploit available and potential employment opportunities.
- Align resources and direct them toward strategic focus areas.
- Enhance efficiency and service delivery in the sector.
- Improve the image and create hope in the minds of the public as centers of work and training excellence.
- Develop and promote the ability of the youth.
- Develop the communities around them.

The major aim of revitalizing the youth polytechnics is to mainstream them into the national vocational training programs. The new curriculum for youth polytechnics will focus on the following programs.

TECHNICAL EDUCATION AND TRAINING IN YOUTH POLYTECHNICS

A 4-year secondary, technical, and vocational education and training programs to absorb primary school leavers who miss places to transit to secondary schooling. This program will provide both theory and practice in the field of science and technology. Successful completion of these programs should lead the graduates to advance to further education at tertiary institutions for either diploma or degree qualifications. It will run parallel to the schooling programs in formal secondary education. This will be a second chance opportunity for those primary school leavers who would otherwise miss secondary education for failing to find places in the current secondary schooling program. The graduates will have to sit for Kenya Certificate of Secondary Education (KCSE) like any other candidates from the formal secondary school.

VOCATIONAL SKILLS EDUCATION AND TRAINING IN YOUTH POLYTECHNICS

The second program will be the core function of the Youth Polytechnics, thus provision of relevant vocational skills that leads directly to self or wage employment. The programs are going to be offered in a modular nature directly geared to performing MSE work activities. Those courses will be offered in level I and II. The learners have to choose and pick the skills demanded by the local industries. Examinations will be offered at the end of level I and II, and those who have graduated successfully will also have the opportunity to proceed to tertiary institutions for either diploma or degree programs.

SHORT SKILL DEVELOPMENT PROGRAMS

The Youth Polytechnics will continue to offer short relevant vocational skills courses, which will be focused to improve already existing skills acquired and new skills required for performing work in the MSE sector. These will include specific enterprise development programs. Some of these programs will be area specific and should enable the learners to develop skills and attitudes that will lead them into income-generating activities in the areas they live in, and so as to improve their standard of living.

At present there are only 13 Youth Polytechnics in all the Muslim ASAL districts in Kenya, out of a national figure of 697 as follows: Moyale 1, Marsabit 2, Isiolo 2, Garissa 3, Mandera 2, Wajir 3. Other districts in the country have between 6 and 20 Youth Polytechnics in each of them.

JUSTIFICATION FOR ESTABLISHING
YOUTH POLYTECHNICS TRAINING PROGRAMS
FOR MUSLIM GIRLS

This study has found that out of 100 secondary education opportunities in North Eastern Province, girls take only nine places. The enrollment of girls in secondary education is just about 27%; this is due to a number of factors, among them being overcrowding in schools, pockets of poverty, inadequate physical facilities, high cost of secondary education, and low quality of education in the few primary schools available in the provinces.

There is low transition rate from primary to secondary education, because there are very few secondary schools in the province, compared to other non-ASAL areas. The situation is exacerbated by gender disparities against girls that affect access retention and academic performance in the schools. The poor performance of girls in national examinations leads to high dropout rates and wastages of important human resources. Gender inequality, with a culture that prejudices girls and women as inferior, has resulted in low enrollment of girls both in primary and secondary education, the community culture that does not allow co-educational schools at the secondary level, especially in boarding and day schools. The community would prefer to send their daughters to "girls-only boarding secondary schools." Currently there are very few girls' boarding secondary schools in these areas because they are expensive to build and maintain.

Education plays an important role in human development by empowering people to improve their well-being and participate actively in nation-building. Education and training help to build human capacity for both men and women; it is a key priority area for poverty reduction by addressing lack of appropriate skills required for earning a livelihood.

Women are more vulnerable to poverty than men; for instance, 69% of active females work as subsistence farmers, compared with 43% of men in Kenya. Subsistence farmers are among the very poor, thus relative dependence of women upon subsistence farming explains the extreme vulnerability of women to poverty. This problem is more severe in ASAL areas, where women have to search for food, water, and fuel to support their families.

Employment statistics in Kenya show that only 29% of the women are engaged in employment activities. Most of the women work in the informal sector where they are ill prepared due to lack of education and training skills. There is also lack of social security and accessibility to credit. The MSE sector has a potential for employment creation and rising of incomes for many families who are participating in the sector. In 2003, the MSE sector created 431,900 jobs, while in 2004 it created 437,000 jobs, showing a higher increase of job creation in the economy.

Youth Polytechnics are now being designed to provide an alternative progression for primary school leavers to technical secondary education and training. As a result of free primary education, 671,550 standard eight pupils sat for the Kenya certificate of primary education (KCPE) in 2005; only 370,589 transited to join secondary education, while 290,961 were expected to join youth polytechnics. The increased number of boarding Youth Polytechnics in the ASAL areas will help to reduce the present wastages of human resources, especially girls.

Youth Polytechnics will provide vocational skills training for self or wage employment or self-employment. Building Youth Polytechnics to absorb Muslim girls in the ASAL areas will empower girls to be economically sustainable and achieve individual aspirations or goals in life.

STUDY RECOMMENDATIONS

- Build appropriate all-girl boarding Youth Polytechnics in each one of the ASAL districts in business-, science-, and mathematics-based subjects and courses. The dispersion of the population in these areas imply that schools are far from the nomadic encampments for the learners to walk long distances in the insecurity-prone areas to go to school and come back the same day. This is one of the causes of low enrollment of children in schools, especially girls.

- Carry out public education by sensitizing parents with a view to improve public attitudes toward schooling.
- Strengthen educational radio programs with specific targets to the nomadic population in ASAL areas.
- Promote parent participation in the school or Youth Polytechnics management.
- In order to improve enrollment rate in secondary education for girls, construct more all-girl boarding schools in ASAL areas. Owing to the problems of poverty and acute food shortage in the region, there is need to strengthen school feeding programs and bursaries to enable the girls from poor families to access and remain in the secondary school sector.
- Establishment of additional Youth Polytechnics in these ASAL areas will enable youth to learn subjects such as animal health, home science, dry land crop production, irrigation, basic human health sciences, business courses including entrepreneurship development, hide and skin production, trading, livestock marketing, rural road construction, and ICT programs.
- There is a need to establish all-girl Youth Polytechnics in almost all the affected ASAL districts such as Wajir, Mandera, and Garissa in North Eastern Province, Moyale Isiolo and Marsabit in Eastern Province, and Tana Rver, Malindi, Kwale, Kilifi, and Lamu in Coast province.
- There is a need for a comprehensive situation-analysis study to determine the real causes of low enrollment and high dropout rates in these ASAL areas, and to adequately coast intervention.

REFERENCES

Okwach Abagi, Status of Education in Kenya, Indicators for Planning and Policy Formulation, IPAR Special Report, December 1997, Nairobi

Republic of Kenya, Poverty Reduction Strategy Paper for the period 2001–2004, Ministry of Finance and Planning, September

UNDP/GOK, The Status of Jua Kali Sheds and Youth Polytechnics in Kenya (Entwise Associates Ltd.), April 2005, Nairobi Kenya

VSO/MED, How to Run a Successful Youth Polytechnic, Micro Enterprise Development Project Pub. IEC Strategy Ltd, 2005, Nairobi, Kenya

GOK/Ministry of State for Youth Affairs, Youth Employment Summit Paper (YES Kenya 2006), September 13–16, 2006, Nairobi, Kenya

UNDP/GOK, Draft National Policy for Youth Polytechnics and Vocational Training Sector (Tharaka Consultancy and General Agencies Ltd.), August 2006, Nairobi Kenya

University of East Angalia and GOK, The Village Polytechnics Training Scheme in Kenya, Ministry of Labour, 1975–80, by Brian Caplan

GOK/Ministry of State for Youth Affairs and UNDP, The Youth YES–MSE Programme Paper, November 2006, Nairobi

Republic of Kenya, Economic Recovery Strategy, Implementation Progress Report 2002.03-06, Prepared by the Ministry of Planning and National Development Gov't Printers, July 2006, Nairobi

United Nations Department of Public and Information, Universal Declaration of Human Rights Paper, November 1988, Nairobi, Kenya

Gargaar Kenya, Concept Paper, on Revitalization of Girl Child Education for Enhanced Community Participation and Improved Academic Standards in Secondary Schools within North Eastern Province

GOK/UNICEF, Situation Analysis of Children and Women in Kenya 1998, UNICEF, Kenya Country Office, Nairobi, 1998

Republic of Kenya, Report of 1998/99 Labour Force Survey, Central Bureau of Statistics Ministry of Planning and Development, Nairobi, March 2003

Republic of Kenya, Geographical Dimensions of Well-being in Kenya Vol. II, Central Bureau of Statistics Ministry of Planning and National Development, Nairobi, 2005

Republic of Kenya and UNDP, Achieving Millennium Development Goals in Kenya, A Needs Assessment and Costing Report, Ministry of Planning and National Development, Nairobi, 2005

UNESCO/ADB (Roy-Carr-Hill), The Education of Nomadic Peoples of East Africa Asynthesis Report, an IIE Study commissioned by the African Development Bank Pub. UNESCO Paris, 2005

Ministry of Education Science and Technology, Education Sector Issues, Challenges, Policies and Strategies, Working Document for the National Forum on Education, Nairobi, 2001

Republic of Kenya, The 1999 Population and Housing Census, Volume I, Central Bureau of Statistics, Ministry of Planning, January 2003, Nairobi, Kenya

Republic of Kenya, Economic Survey 2005, Central Bureau of Statistics, Ministry of Planning and National Development, Government Printer, Nairobi 2005

List of the Persons Interviewed Who Gave Useful Information for the Study

Name	Organization
1. Mr. Idris Farah	The Supreme Council of Kenya Muslims (SUPKEM) former Deputy Director of Education Ministry of Education
2. Mr. Yusuf Murabwa	SUPKEM member
3. Mr. Hassan Ole Naado	SUPKEM muslim youth leader
4. Mr. Bakary Chemaswet	SUPKEM Member
5. Dr. Esther Kakonge	Secretary General Kenya National Commission to UNESCO
6. Mrs. Nuriya S. Farah	Gargaar Kenya (Muslim Women Education NGO) North Eastern Province
7. Mr. Noor Hassan	North Eastern Provincial Technical Education Officer, Ministry of Labour
8. Mr. John Lodiaga	Programme Officer, Aga Khan Foundation (Education Services) East Africa, Mombasa
9. Mr. Elias Jama Noor	Assistant Project Officer, Education and Youth Fund UNICEF (KCO) Nairobi
10. Prof. Hyder Matano	Consultant Islamic Education Programme Mombasa
11. Dr. Ahdija Shikali	Provincial Medical Officer Muslim Women Education Campaigner (Mombasa)
12. Mrs. Karim	Former Provincial Director of Education Coast Province Mombasa
13. Mrs. Dekkar	Dekkar Muslim Education Foundation Mombasa
14. Mrs. Abida Ali	Lawyer, former Chairperson Kenya, Constitutional Review Commission, Nairobi
15. Mr. Mohammed Atrash	Dekkar Muslim Education Foundation Mombasa
16. Mr. Seif Bandera	Dekkar Muslim Education Foundation Mombasa

Printed in the United States
200490BV00018B/1/A

9 781593 117696